Making a Scene

Kimberly A. Creasap

Making a Scene

Urban Landscapes, Gentrification,

and Social Movements in Sweden

TEMPLE UNIVERSITY PRESS

Philadelphia • *Rome* • *Tokyo*

TEMPLE UNIVERSITY PRESS
Philadelphia, Pennsylvania 19122
tupress.temple.edu

Library of Congress Cataloging-in-Publication Data

Names: Creasap, Kimberly A., 1978– author.
Title: Making a scene : urban landscapes, gentrification, and social
  movements in Sweden / Kimberly A. Creasap.
Description: Philadelphia : Temple University Press, 2022. | Includes
  bibliographical references and index. | Summary: "This book compares the
  landscapes of three Swedish cities to show how urban geography affects
  the place-making efforts of local activists looking to push back against
  encroaching gentrification. The centrality, concentration, and
  visibility of a movement scene impacts the movement's ability to
  effectively claim a space"— Provided by publisher.
Identifiers: LCCN 2021022995 (print) | LCCN 2021022996 (ebook) |
  ISBN 9781439920879 (cloth) | ISBN 9781439920886 (paperback) |
  ISBN 9781439920893 (pdf)
Subjects: LCSH: Public spaces—Sweden. | City and town life—Sweden. |
  Social movements—Sweden. | Social action—Sweden. |
  Gentrification—Social aspects—Sweden. | Counterculture—Sweden. |
  Sweden—Social conditions—21st century.
Classification: LCC HT178.S8 C74 2022 (print) | LCC HT178.S8 (ebook) |
  DDC 307.7609485—dc23
LC record available at https://lccn.loc.gov/2021022995
LC ebook record available at https://lccn.loc.gov/2021022996

Dedicated to Arlene Binns—
thank you for being a model of lifelong learning
and inspiring me to be curious
about the world.

Contents

Acknowledgments   ix

1 Introduction   1
2 Uniquely Swedish: From Social Democracy to Autonomy   28
3 Social Centers: Where Past, Present, and Future Meet   47
4 City Solidarity: The Right to the City in Malmö   81
5 Where Is the Movement? The Spatiality of Social
   Movement Scenes   109
6 The Future of Place-Based Movements   148

Appendix: Methods and Access   157
Bibliography   163
Index   179

Acknowledgments

This book had a long incubation period. Because it has been a long road, I have many people to thank.

I began this book as a graduate student at the University of Pittsburgh, and I was lucky to have an excellent team of mentors, supporters, and friends. Thank you to John Markoff, Annulla Linders, Todd Reeser, Jean Carr, and many other faculty who championed my work as a graduate student. There are not enough words to express the respect and admiration I have for my graduate advisor, Kathleen Blee. I continue to look up to her fifteen years after meeting her for the first time. Thank you for encouraging my development as a writer. As one of Kathy's advisees, I had the good fortune to participate in a qualitative writing workshop, and my peers in that group read numerous drafts of what eventually became book chapters. Big thanks to Ashley Currier, Lisa Huebner, Elizabeth Yates, and especially Kelsy Burke, Brittany Duncan, Yolanda Hernandez-Albujar, Amy McDowell, Marie Skoczylas, and Jane Walsh for your incisive comments, friendship, and support at various stages of my career.

Suzanne Staggenborg has also remained a steadfast supporter and mentor. I owe her a special debt of gratitude for connecting me with Ryan Mulligan, my editor at Temple University Press. Ryan has been a joy to work with and a steadfast motivator to keeping the book moving forward.

During my fieldwork, I benefitted from Swedish scholars Stellan Vinthagen, Adrienne Sörbom, Kerstin Jacobsson, and Ove Sernhede as they connected me with activists, shared insights from their work, and helped me secure visiting research positions at Södertörns högskola and Göteborgs Universitet. I am also grateful for the kindness and generosity of two dear friends, Johanna Lindkvist and Karin Ekberg, who housed, fed, and listened to me during the trials and tribulations of fieldwork. *Stort tack till er alla.*

I am grateful to have found nurturing academic communities at Colgate University, Wake Forest University, and Denison University. I worked with more wonderful colleagues at these institutions than I have space to thank them, so here is a short list: Meika Loe, Carolyn Hsu, Travis Beaver, Ashley Taylor, Joseph Soares, Amanda Gengler, Amanda Vincent, Brooke Coe, Chelsea Wentworth Fournier, Erik Farley, Léna Crain, Stephanie Jackson, and Laurel Kennedy. Thank you for your encouragement, guidance, mentorship, camaraderie, and critical reading of my work. Many thanks also to my wonderful undergraduate research assistant, Smelanda Jean-Baptiste, and graphic designer extraordinaire, Whitley Trusler. Your patience, keen intellectual insights, and attention to detail in helping me prepare this manuscript are so appreciated.

Finally, I am lucky to have loving family and friends who have listened to and encouraged me during every stage of writing this book. Erin Byrne, Sherice Clarke, and Jodi Creasap Gee have supported and cheered me on through the tough work of writing, revising, submitting proposals, job searching, moving around the country, and enduring a global pandemic. Thank you most of all to Alan, Lauren, Tyler, and Bruce Creasap for making me laugh throughout the writing process; Cynthia Binns, whose tenacious spirit continues to inspire me; and John and Arlene Binns for sparking my curiosity about the larger world, teaching me to never give up, and sharing your stories with me.

Making a Scene

1

Introduction

Stockholm Is Destroyed
The Battle over Göteborg
Stop Gentrification in Möllevången (Malmö)

These are the messages that I encountered on leaflets, posters, and banners as I traveled through the cafés, bookstores, social centers, and squats created by autonomous left-wing movements in Sweden's major cities. Cities were formidable battlefields for the competing forces of capitalism, government regulation, and activism. Gentrification was the enemy, turning activists into amateur urban planners, architects, builders, and neighborhood association leaders to create more participatory, democratic neighborhoods. Yet I did not visibly encounter activism in either Stockholm or Göteborg with any regularity. In contrast, Malmö activists had visibly marked "their" territory with spray paint, stickers, and graffiti. These visual markings on the streets, sidewalks, and walls indicated a social movement presence and served as a set of territorial boundaries

A portion of Chapter 1 appears in Kimberly Creasap, "Social Movement Scenes: Place-Based Politics and Everyday Resistance," *Sociology Compass* 6:2, January 25, 2012. John Wiley and Sons.

drawn by activists to denote that the battle for the neighborhood was under way. On a summer day in June, I ventured out for a walk through Möllevången, a neighborhood in central Malmö, Sweden. The neighborhood is anchored by Folkets Park (the People's Park) on its northeastern edge, so I took a bus to the park entrance to begin my stroll. A placard at the entrance explains that the park was purchased by the Social Democratic Party in 1891 as a place for political speeches, recreation, and demonstration. This park was also intended to provide nineteenth-century laborers a retreat from polluted factories and cramped housing. The Social Democratic history of the park was evident as I passed through the gates. I was immediately drawn to a large fountain in the shape of a pink rose (the rose is a symbol of Social Democracy), where children splashed as their parents chatted among one another. A series of concrete busts dot the landscape: Per Albin Hansson, a prominent architect of the Social Democratic Party during the 1920s and '30s stands proudly next to people lounging on picnic blankets. Olof Palme, leader of the Social Democratic Party from 1969 until his assassination in 1986, stands silently among the trees.

I exited the park and walked on the streets of Möllevången with no real destination in mind. Planned as a residential neighborhood for industrial workers in the early twentieth century, Möllan, as locals call it, is characterized by the kind of solid, blocky buildings that one commonly sees in former working-class districts in Sweden—concrete, heavy, and drably colored in shades of goldenrod, olive green, and brown brick. A wall along the park's edge was plastered with posters for events and concerts, but I was most intrigued by one that read, "Stop the Gentrification of Möllevången." As I walked farther along the street, I came across a spray-painted message on the sidewalk: "Isolate Israel.now" (*Isolera Israel.nu*) and made a note to look it up when I got home (it turned out to be a network aimed at leading boycotts and sanctions against Israel in favor of a free Palestine; see BDS Sweden 2014). A drainpipe bore an Anti-Fascist Action (AFA) sticker. Another poster announced the upcoming Möllevångsfestivalen, a street festival celebrating socialism and environmentalism with "red" and "green" coded streets, respectively.

I stopped for coffee at Glassfabriken, a café housed in a former ice cream factory. The political character of the café was evident everywhere. More of the large, colorful flyers inside the front door called on visitors to "Stop the Gentrification of Möllevången." Racks of magazines with titles such as *Direkt Aktion* (Direct Action) lined the walls. The cash register was covered with stickers that read "Love Animals, Don't Eat Them" and "These faggots bash back," mixing the messages of animal rights and queer activism. A library along the back wall contained anti-capitalist manifestos: *No Logo* and *The Shock Doctrine* by Naomi Klein.

As I sipped my coffee, I reflected on how social movements were inscribed on the landscape of Möllevången. Taken alone, this experience might not have been particularly surprising. However, I had spent months in Stockholm and Göteborg, Sweden's two largest cities, trying to learn about urban social movements. Based on what I had read online, both cities seemed to have vibrant, active urban movements. While I observed consistent squatting actions, demonstrations, and conversations around urban space, they were scattered, temporary, and difficult to find.

In Möllevången, urban space was visibly marked with the signs and symbols of social movements, both past and present. A network of urban activists was connected through a network of physical spaces: Glassfabriken, the social centers Utkanten and Kontrapunkt, a radical feminist bookshop called Amalthea, the local neighborhood association, and more—all within walking distance of one another. The more I frequented these places, the more I saw the same people repeatedly, even bumping into them on the streets. These networks were also centrally located, meaning they were not difficult to find or access, so many different people encountered social movements in the same way that I had.

My walk through the streets of Möllevången made me question how urban movements are spatially constructed in their local environments. The visible, concentrated activism of Möllevången in central Malmö was a stark contrast to the scattered and temporary actions I had observed in the Göteborg and Stockholm suburbs. How do different urban settings affect the spatial dimensions of social movements? Why are some movements embedded in the urban landscape while others struggle to leave a mark?

This book charts the spatial dimensions of social movements and the urban conditions under which they thrive or fade. My research revealed that gentrification was key to understanding the spatial strategies of urban movements. On one hand, gentrification sharpened social movement grievances and led many activists to becoming expert planners, builders, and neighborhood association leaders. On the other, rising rents, changes in local amenities, and battles with authorities eventually destroyed the conditions under which these movements thrived. This book centers *social movement scenes* as structures of resistance. For social movements that promote a subcultural or countercultural way of life, social movement scenes are crucial for understanding social movement momentum and vitality. A *social movement scene* is "a *network of people* who share a set of subcultural or countercultural beliefs, values, norms, and convictions as well as *a network of physical spaces* where members of that group are known to congregate" (Leach and Haunss 2009, 260, emphasis in the original). In this book, the network of people consists of loosely organized and ideologically varied networks called *autonomous social movements*. The ideological variety is evident in symbols dotting the streets of Malmö: anti-capitalist, anti-fascist, anti-gentrification, queer, and animal rights activists are all part of the scene. The autonomous movements in this book are *urban movements*, not only because they operate in urban areas but because their efforts focus on how city space is used and by whom.

Centering scenes in my analysis differs from sociological social movement scholarship, in which scenes are cast as pools of mobilization for "real" activism and auxiliary to social movements. I argue that the production of scenes *is* activism for urban movements, not a precursor to it. Scenes are where many urban movements experiment with creating participatory, democratic cities. Through the production of social movement scenes, urban movements seek to change the built environment, social fabric of neighborhoods, and local political processes. For example, during Möllevångsfestivalen, an annual street festival in Möllevången that people considered part of the scene, activists installed living room furniture on the streets and sidewalks. Residents moved their own sofas, chairs, coffee tables, and rugs into the streets—some even included water bowls for pets. This changed the built environment, transforming the streets and sidewalks from pathways for pedestrians and cars into places you wanted to sit down and enjoy with friends. It also brought the social fabric of the neighborhood into full view. Möllevången was the kind of neighborhood where people stopped and chatted through open windows or while passing each other on the street. When the streets became a giant living room, we all got to feel that same social connectedness that residents felt in their everyday lives. Prompted by activists, this action spread through the neighborhood, giving their neighbors an opportunity to "reclaim their streets" and create participatory spaces for imagining the future of the neighborhood.

Interviews with thirty-eight autonomous activists and fourteen months of ethnographic observations capture the social dynamics of scenes, while comparative case analysis reveals some of the driving factors for why scenes thrive or fizzle in different urban environments. Differing configurations of social movement scenes are partially shaped by the structural conditions of the cities in which they form. Malmö activists felt emotionally connected to a particular neighborhood because of its labor movement history, carefree character, rich cultural life, and sociocultural heterogeneity. The threats posed by gentrification of the area energized autonomous movements. Their efforts were aimed at solidifying their place (as residents and as activists) in a unique neighborhood that they loved. In Stockholm and Göteborg, analogous neighborhoods gentrified decades ago. Social movements no longer had a place in the physical and social landscape of central Stockholm and were fleeting in Göteborg.

Gentrification and the Swedish Welfare State

Sweden is a strategic place for studying urban movement scenes for two reasons. First, advanced welfare states are more conducive to the development of social movement scenes (Leach and Haunss 2009). In societies where unemployment insurance and healthcare are not dependent on employment status and the cost of education does not create a lifetime of debt, full-time engagement in radical politics is more possible. Second, Swedish housing policy presents a unique hybrid of strong government regulation and free market competition. This constrains urban movements in terms of "do-it-yourself" styles of building but also forces them to be tactically innovative. Additionally, unlike some European countries that recognized squatters' rights in response to housing shortages after World War II, Sweden was neutral during the war, so squatting and claiming space without permission has never been legal. As more countries evict social movements from their spaces and places, perhaps the Swedish cases can provide some tactical inspiration. Though the image of Sweden as a social democratic paradise persists in the minds of many scholars, this is a stereotype based on outdated notions of the Swedish welfare state. To outside observers, it might seem that a strong welfare state like Sweden would slow the process of gentrification. The modern Swedish housing system was established by a "strong welfare state with cheap high-quality housing through subsidized construction, strong tenant protections, high formal demands on quality standards, and collectively negotiated rent levels" (Baeten et al. 2017, 636). Affordable "housing for all" was a pillar of Swedish social democracy when the government began "The Million Program" (Miljonprogrammet), an ambitious plan to address housing shortages by constructing one million new dwellings over a ten-year period (1965–1974).[1] The program exceeded its goal, leading many scholars to characterize the housing system as yet another "success" of Swedish social democracy (Baeten et al. 2017; Christophers 2013; Hedin et al. 2012).

Constructing new housing stock meant demolishing thousands of inner-city homes to make room for new ones. In the late 1960s, grassroots urban movements (*byalagsrörelsen*) began to protest demolitions and the wave of housing displacement they created (Franzén 2005; Stahre 1999). The political economy of housing—and Swedish cities more generally—shifted in the early 1970s. Rent regulations were lifted, making urban housing markets competitive (Franzén 2005), and a national economic crisis began the process of welfare retrenchment (Thörn and Thörn 2017). In the absence of state funding, cities used entrepreneurial strategies to find new funding sources and turned to market-based solutions. These shifts created a "monstrous hybrid" of government regulations and neoliberal policy, deepening socioeconomic segregation (Christophers 2013) and fomenting resistance from urban movements.

---

1. For a discussion on the transformations of everyday life in the Million Program areas, see Kärrholm and Wirdelöv 2019.

Gentrification began in Stockholm's city center in the early 1970s (Franzén 2005), Göteborg in the 1980s (H. Thörn 2012), and Malmö in the early 2000s (see Chapter 4). Comparing scenes in these three cities allows us to see how, on one hand, gentrification creates opportunities for urban social movements to claim territory and experiment with "spatial justice." On the other hand, gentrification disrupts and eventually destroys the urban environments these movements need to thrive. The Malmö case was paradigmatic of a scene that thrived for years in a gentrifying neighborhood. Activists predicted (correctly) that the scene would eventually fizzle, but they used the scene to appropriate space and create opportunities for residents to participate in shaping the future of their neighborhood. In this way, social movement scenes are promising structures for challenging neoliberal urbanism, characterized by large-scale urban development, entrepreneurial governance, privatization of infrastructures and services, and social inequalities (Harvey 2012; Mayer 2016).

Social Movement Scenes: A Conceptual Framework

There has been little "cross-fertilization" between geographical and sociological analyses of social movements; what does exist is mainly the work of geographers studying collective action rather than sociological analyses of spatiality (Martin 2015, 153). Even *within* sociology, urban movement research remains rather separate from "mainstream" social movement studies. Just as a social movement scene is a constellation of places that form a coherent whole, my conceptualization of a social movement scene is an interdisciplinary collage of scholarship in cultural studies, sociology, geography, and urban studies. I begin laying out a conceptual framework for social movement scenes with a discussion of how this concept contributes to scholarship on social movement cultures. Then, I turn my attention to a discussion of how the concept contributes to sociospatial perspectives in geographical and urban studies scholarship.

My theoretical contributions to understanding social movement scenes are twofold: first, I argue that scholars should analyze the production of social movement scenes in order to better understand how urban social movements shape and are shaped by their local environments. This contrasts with the work of scholars who have examined the auxiliary role that scenes play as easy access points for movements (Leach and Haunss 2009) or as pools of mobilization (Allen and Miles 2020). Second, I add conceptual specificity to the concept of a scene by examining three dimensions of scenes: centrality, concentration, and visibility.

Social Movement Cultures

Beginning with the Chicago School in the early twentieth century, sociologists have explored micro-worlds ranging from gangs to dance halls, punk clubs to discos, and jazz clubs to gothic music scenes. Sociologist John Irwin (1973, 1977) undertook the first attempt to conceptualize scenes, first in a journal article about surfing and later in a book. Scholars have used the concept of a "scene" to study expressive, lifestyle scenes, focusing on style, consumerism, leisure, and aesthetics (see Bennett and Kahn-Harris 2004; Bennett and Peterson 2004; Hall and Jefferson 1975; Hebdige 1979; Irwin 1977; Lloyd 2006; Muggleton 2005; Muggleton and Weinzierl 2003; and Straw 2004). In the 1990s, a small group of cultural studies scholars advocated a theoretical shift from studying subcultures, which they viewed as static and homogeneous, to a study of something more dynamic (see, e.g., Bennett and Kahn-Harris 2004; Hesmondhalgh 2005; and Muggleton and Weinzierl 2003). These scholars emphasize the "sociospatial aspects" of scenes—"allusions to flexibility and transience, of temporary, ad hoc and strategic associations, a cultural space notable as much for its restricted as well as its porous sociality, its connotations of flux and flow, movement and mutability"—and made the concept more appealing for capturing the dynamics of these micro-worlds (Stahl 2004, 53).

Using the concept of a scene as a starting point, sociologists Darcy Leach and Sebastian Haunss (2009, 260) coined the term "social movement scene" (see also Creasap 2012, 2016). Not all social movements develop scenes. Scenes are important to movements "for whom defending, creating, and/or promoting a marginalized, repressed, or countercultural way of life is an essential aspect of their political praxis" (Leach and Haunss 2009, 273). In Europe and the United States, these include radical feminist, gay and lesbian, and anarchist movements on the political left and white power skinhead and neo-Nazi movements on the political right (Simi and Futrell 2010).

Scholars of new social movements have described social movement cultures using terms such as "free spaces" (Couto 1993; Evans and Boyte 1992; Polletta 1999), "submerged networks" (Melucci 1989), "safe spaces" (Gamson 1997), and "cultural havens," among others (Fantasia and Hirsch 1995). Free spaces are "small-scale settings within a community or movement that are removed from the direct control of dominant groups, are voluntarily participated in, and generate the cultural challenge that precedes or accompanies political mobilization" (Polletta 1999, 1). As Leach and Haunss (2009) point out, a social movement scene shares characteristics with these ideas, but there is little uniformity in how the structures of these cultural spaces are defined. Some analyses refer to single places (Chatterton 2010; Glass 2010), while others include cyber networks (Kahn and Kellner 2004) and/or informal parties (Simi and Futrell 2010). Leach and Haunss (2009, 259) have written a lengthy discussion distinguishing scenes from these other concepts, particularly free spaces. They conclude that a scene can be described as "a network of free spaces that encompasses one or more subcultures and/or countercultures." This is what sociologist Walter Nicholls (2009, 88) refers to as "places of resistance strung together to form a relatively coherent social movement space." According to these definitions, social centers, infoshops, and coffeehouses are individual free spaces. The relationships, events, and activities that connect these spaces are what constitute a scene. Therefore, a single place would not constitute a scene. A scene must include several places that are in some way connected to one another and to social movements.

Leach and Haunss (2009) offer a compelling start to the study of social movement scenes, but they tend to paint a picture of a rather stable entity and focus on what functions scenes serve for social movements, such as fostering mobilization, providing a point of entry into a movement, and whether scenes help or hinder a movement's political and/or cultural influence. While their definition of a scene as networks of people and places is useful and scenes may well benefit movements in the ways they describe, I propose that thinking of scenes as *processes* is more useful than thinking of them solely as stable contexts where political activity happens (Creasap 2012, 2016). The dynamic energy and movement evoked by the term "scene" is what prompted scholars to move away from models of subculture, which tend to be overly structural and insufficiently interactional, and toward a study of scenes (Bennett and Kahn-Harris 2004). Scenes are works in progress. They are never final but always coming and going. The processes of "making a scene"—through challenges to who "belongs" in public (and in some cases, private) spaces, rituals like music and protest, and everyday practices—*are* political work. This is not to say that the scene is the *entire* movement; not all people who participate in movements necessarily hang out in the scene. Conversely, not all people who hang out in the scene identify as part of a movement. Scenes and movements *intersect*, but they are not one and the same (Creasap 2012; Haunss and Leach 2007).

The concept of a scene shares commonalities with the concept of a social movement community (SMC) (Staggenborg 1998, 2013) but differs in important ways. Like SMCs, scenes are conceptually useful for "look[ing] for movements in a wide variety of places" (Staggenborg 2013, 141). The conceptual distinction between SMCs and scenes is an emphasis on territoriality and spatial dynamics. SMCs are "not necessarily territorial, but [involve] human relations, which may be maintained through social networks rather than physical locale" (Staggenborg 1998, 182). For urban social movements, place is deeply important for structuring social interactions, relationships, and social movement action. Part of how they understand their collective identity is as inhabitants of a neighborhood or city, so territorial claims are vitally important to their movements (Creasap 2016). The concept of a social movement scene, which includes a network of places as a fundamental element, allows scholars to attend to the effects of the spatial arrangements of social movements.

Scenes also share some features of "abeyance structures" (Taylor 1989), but not always. Abeyance refers to "a holding process by which movements sustain themselves in nonreceptive political environments and provide continuity from one stage of mobilization to another" (Taylor 1989, 761). This idea applies in the case of Stockholm, where activists talked about needing places to sustain the collective energy generated in temporary spaces and at one-off events. But in the case of Malmö, the idea of an abeyance structure does not fit. The idea of a "holding process" between mobilizations assumes that public challenges to authority (e.g., demonstrations, legislative challenges) are what constitute activism. Urban movements operate under the assumption that creating new ways of everyday life *is* activism. This was especially the case in Malmö, where the scene helped movements make activism a part of everyday life. In this way, scenes facilitated *ongoing* activism, not only a structure that facilitated mass mobilizations or provided a means of being involved in a movement between periods of protest activity.

As structures that may be fleeting *or* that last for years, scenes are also temporally defined. Social movements in this book draw on the histories of social movements, express urgency about their places in the present, and seek to build strong scenes in order to create *reach*— a temporal extension into the future. A group's orientation to the future—even if that future does not come true—shapes action in the present (Blee 2012, 2013; Creasap 2020; Emirbayer and Mische 1998; Mische 2009). As sites of experimentation and deliberation, social movement scenes provide many opportunities to observe "'sites of hyper-projectivity,' that is, arenas of heightened, future-oriented public debate about contending futures" (Mische 2014, 438). For example, *volition* refers to motion in relation to the future; do groups see themselves as moving toward the future (e.g., active agents of change, as in Malmö) or do they see the future as moving toward them (e.g., responding to a crisis, as in Göteborg)? Orientation to these dimensions of projectivity shapes action and, in turn, shapes the scene.

Taking Up Space

The Right to the City

Rooted in the work of French social theorist Henri Lefebvre ([1968] 1996), sociospatial perspectives on social movements integrate analyses of social life with political economies of cities (see Domaradzka 2018; Harvey 2012; Martin 2015; Martínez López 2018; Nicholls, Miller, and Beaumont 2013; and Yip, López, and Sun 2019 for overviews). Lefebvre recognized that urban movements, for which "the transformation of daily urban life" was a goal, are crucial to imagining and remaking urban space (Harvey 2012, xvi). In Lefebvrian terms, social movement scenes are *perceived spaces*—space as it is experienced in everyday life by inhabitants. Lefebvre argued that the city itself is an *oeuvre*, a work of art collectively forged by humans throughout its history; the "artists" are urban residents and their everyday routines. This view of the urban, Lefebvre argued, conflicts with the modern capitalist city, where "the corporate system regulates the distribution of actions and activities over urban space (streets and neighborhoods)" (Lefebvre [1968] 1996, 68). Lefebvre does not define the right to political participation in terms of national citizenship, elected officials, or the structures of state and local governments; it is those who *inhabit* urban communities—what he calls *citadins* (a combination of citizen and denizen)—who should have a voice in all decisions that affect the production of urban space. Lefebvre does not explicitly state that inhabitants should entirely and solely make decisions about their communities, but the right to the city "would give urban inhabitants a literal seat at the corporate table" (Purcell 2002, 102; see also Attoh 2011 and Gilbert and Dikeç 2008).

Social movement scenes, produced by activists by appropriating space and creating opportunities for democratic forms of participation, are an expression of the right to the city. According to Lefebvre ([1968] 1996), city inhabitants have two main rights: the right to *participation* in the production of urban space and the right to *appropriation* of urban space. The former is relatively straightforward; city inhabitants should be able to participate fully in any decision-making processes that involve city space. The right of appropriation relies on a Marxist distinction between *use value* and *exchange value*, calling on inhabitants to prioritize a city's use value (satisfying human needs or desires) over its exchange value (a commodity for exchange). This distinction becomes muddied in the context of entrepreneurial urbanism, where culture and creativity—which are, to some extent, satisfying for human desires—become marketable (Florida 2002, 2013, 2017). Unlike previous well-known cultural districts (e.g., Montmartre in Paris, SoHo in New York), which "emerged spontaneously from currents of dissent, conflict, and collision," contemporary cultural districts are "sequestered in artificially-created zone[s]" by city officials (Leslie 2005, 405). In order to stay competitive in a post-industrial era, city governments must do whatever they can to attract wealthy investors, residents, tourists, and developers (Bryson 2013).

Critical scholars regard such entrepreneurial strategies as gentrification with a cool, artsy façade (Peck 2005; Slater 2006; Bryson 2013). Gentrification is "a gradual process, occurring one block or one building at a time, slowly reconfiguring the neighborhood landscape of consumption and residence" (Pérez 2004, 139). New amenities designed to attract young, urbane professionals become progenitors of commercial gentrification (Lees 2003). Many scholarly studies focus on the effects of gentrification, such as displacement of poor and working-class residents (Betancur 2011; Levy, Comey, and Padilla 2006; Newman and Wyly 2006; Pérez 2004), changes in housing tenure (Hedin et al. 2012; Watt 2009), or adaptive reuse of old buildings for upscale commercial places (Wang 2011; Zukin et al. 2009). Fewer studies examine how people who live in gentrifying neighborhoods resist these changes (for notable exceptions, see Annunziata and Rivas-Alonso 2020; King and Lowe 2018; and Pearsall 2013).

Studying scenes requires attention to the tight interplay between how movement actors construct scenes *and* the political, social, and cultural environments in which they operate. For example, the relationship between urban movements and gentrification depends on local political dynamics (Martínez 2020). A study of squatting in Amsterdam and New York indicates that squatters spurred gentrification early on by making visible claims on territory and generating media attention (Pruijt 2003). The culture that urban movements create in a neighborhood can then be framed by urban developers to appeal to creative middle- and upper-class professionals. Squatters in these cases mitigated these effects by siding with original inhabitants to fight development efforts; although movement actors may have more social and cultural capital than other neighborhood residents, they often share a lack of economic capital that can serve as a source of solidarity (Pruijt 2003). This did not stop gentrification but may have slowed the process. In the Prenzlauer Berg neighborhood in East Berlin, squatters sought legalization of their spaces after the fall of the Berlin Wall, thereby securing their place in the neighborhood at an advantageous time. Although squatters opposed gentrification, they worked with the city government in order to maintain and secure their status as legal squats. In doing so, they secured rents well below market price, which slowed gentrification in the area (Holm and Kuhn 2017). These examples show just how crucial timing, relationships, and local political contexts are to the effects of urban social movements.

Social movement scenes throughout Europe have become increasingly fragile as a result of neoliberal urbanism that characterizes twenty-first-century cities. Since the mid-2000s, autonomous movements in Copenhagen, Amsterdam, and Berlin have been evicted from squatted social centers by city authorities to make way for commercial ventures (Creasap 2012; Martínez 2020). As a result, autonomous movements have been fighting to maintain their place in the urban landscape. For these movements, there is more at stake than cheap real estate (though this is certainly important). Autonomous movements take space in protest of the "corporate city," which represents "the high end of growth, the cultural hegemony of finance and the standardization of individual desire" (Zukin 2009, 545). Social movement scenes represent a return to the "urban village . . . the low-key and often low-income neighborhood, the culture of ethnic and social class solidarity, and the dream of restoring a ruptured community" (Zukin 2009, 546). Autonomous responses to gentrification and privatization of public space are both symbolic (a rejection of corporate values) and practical (offering an affordable alternative to consumers or residents). Taking up space in these neighborhoods is viewed by activists as a means of reclaiming (or protecting) deindustrialized, working-class neighborhoods from corporate housing developers and/or governmental control.

Spatial Dimensions of Scenes

Sociospatial perspectives, found in a rich body of geographical and urban studies research on social movements, are necessary for understanding scenes as spatial entities. Urban sociologists, geographers, and historians have produced much work about what we can call social movement scenes, using Leach and Haunss's (2009) definition. However, many of these examples offer "descriptors for some form of provisional unity" (Anderson and McFarlane 2011, 125) rather than conceptualizations of sociospatial structures. Scholars of the American feminist movement of the 1970s have shown how the movement inhabited networks of free spaces in American cities, including bars, bookstores, parks, health clinics, and rape crisis centers (Enke 2007; Spain 2016). Scholarship on contemporary labor movements shows how "labor and community coalitions move outside the workplace to social halls, church basements, and pubs to organize around issues of joint concern" (Greenberg and Lewis 2017). Historian Tom Goyens (2009, 445) describes "seemingly ordinary places [that] were, in effect, a network, an alternative space carved in the dominant, capitalist space of the metropolis" by German anarchists living in New York in the early twentieth century. Italian sociologist Vincenzo Ruggiero (2001, 112) paints a clear picture of a scene as "participating in the same events and, at times, sharing specific places and spaces in the city . . . [including] small 'alternative' restaurants, coffee shops, bookshops, bars, [and] also just squares and junctions." Even though these scholars do not use the term "scene," these descriptions include politically like-minded people (autonomists, labor activists, feminists, anarchists) who frequent a network of physical places that are in some way cultural "alternatives." These examples show that scenes are important to spatial analyses of social movements, but—as is the case in social movement studies—lack uniformity in how these structures are defined (see also Arampatzi 2017).

Scenes share some conceptual ground with geographical assemblages. "Assemblage" refers broadly to "a composition of diverse elements [that] form [a] provisional socio-spatial formation" (Anderson and McFarlane 2011, 124; see also Deleuze and Guattari 1987; Davies 2012; and McFarlane 2009). A social movement scene, then, is an assemblage of places, movements, and activists that form a coherent structure. However, the word "provisional" is key in the definition of an assemblage because it indicates a temporal element as well as a spatial one (Anderson and McFarlane 2011). Part of the conceptual promise of a "scene" lies in its malleability, flow, and flux; elements of a scene—like those of movements—coalesce, disperse, realign, move, and morph.

An important contribution of this book is to add specificity to the concept of a social movement scene. Specifically, I present three dimensions of scenes in this book: *centrality* (relative to the central business district), *concentration* (clustering of scene places in one area of the city), and *visibility* (a visible presence communicated by signs and symbols). Geographers and urban studies scholars have written about networks of places ranging from town squares to coffeehouses to softball fields (see, e.g., Enke 2007; Greenberg and Lewis

2017; and Spain 2016), but these tend to be mainly descriptive rather than conceptual, leaving many questions about how to think about scenes as spatial structures. Shaped by social movements and the political economies of cities, scenes vary along each of these dimensions to produce different scene structures. These dimensions and scene structures are based on deductive analysis of existing scene studies and inductive analysis of my research on social movement scenes in Swedish cities. These dimensions are not exhaustive, but they add specificity to the concept while remaining dynamic enough to apply to a wide variety of scene structures and locales.

Concentration is important for any type of scene. Scenes are networks of people and places. Therefore, proximity creates opportunities for different people and groups to interact with one another *and* "a stable base exists for repeated collaborations" (Nicholls 2009, 84). However, the relative importance of centrality and visibility differs in other local contexts. These dimensions, which are rooted in territoriality and power, are especially important for understanding scenes in changing neighborhoods. In gentrifying neighborhoods, several groups—original inhabitants, new inhabitants, developers, activists, property owners, city authorities—battle for territorial control.

Centrality refers to proximity to the central business district (CBD) of a city. City centers are "commercial, religious, intellectual, political and economic" hubs that draw people from the suburbs and beyond (Lefebvre [1968] 1996, 73). In changing neighborhoods, urban movements seek to change the built environment, social fabric, and political processes of cities, making proximity to centers of decision making crucial. Pragmatically, centrality allows greater access to meeting places and activities. European squatting movements "aim at locating [squatted social centers] in the most convenient buildings and urban areas for people to gather, meet, and develop activities . . . [When] squatting for housing, the centrality issue may be less relevant" (Martínez López 2018, 13; see also Adinolfi 2019). By contrast, Parisian autonomous social centers are in the city's eastern suburbs. Strategically, Parisian movements sought to "maintain a maximum distance from the state as well as from the institutional way of living in urban spaces. As a result, they are hostile to public authorities, considering them their major enemy" (Aguilera 2018, 131). In this case, centrality is strategically avoided by the group. This is a good example of how social movement strategy is tightly linked with local environments.

Visibility refers to a scene with a visible presence indicated by signs and symbols. In gentrifying neighborhoods, a number of groups wage territorial and discursive battles to define a neighborhood as "theirs." In the absence of formal control, visibly marking territory is a way of claiming space (see, e.g., De Backer 2019 and Pecile 2017). For autonomous movements, this includes claiming territory with fly-posting, graffiti, stickers, and activist-produced media. In a study of fly-posting in Rome and Berlin, sociologist Paulo Gerbaudo (2014) writes that "fly-posting in the autonomous scene should be understood fundamentally as a practice of diffuse boundary-making, constructing a sense of antagonistic territoriality around the movement strongholds" (246).[2] Through these practices, autonomous movements lay claim to walls, streets, and squares. These practices are often illegal. In Hamburg, Germany, autonomous movements in the central neighborhood Sternschanze used a "de-attraction" strategy aimed at showing would-be gentrifiers that they were not welcome. They used "arson and vandalism . . . against . . . symbols of capitalist wealth" like new shops, condominiums, chain restaurants, and banks in order to promote a negative image of the neighborhood to potential gentrifiers (Naegler 2012, 81). This also had the effect of making visible, even spectacular, claims on territory. These actions signaled that the rules and laws of the city did not matter to activists because they claimed the territory as their own, rejecting property rights and state control of public space. An effect of gentrification is that groups threatened with displacement must fight for visibility even more (Pell 2014).

"Why Sweden?" Welfare Retrenchment and Neoliberal Urbanism

The question I am asked most frequently about this research is "why Sweden?" People ask this question for a variety of reasons ranging

---

2. See also Gibril (2018) for a similar discussion on the use of graffiti and street art during the Egyptian Revolution.

from curiosity to skepticism. The curious want to know about the people and character of a small, northern nation with a reputation for beauty and equality. The skeptics question what kind of grievances social movements might have in such a place. In response, I often find myself quoting the late geographer Allan Pred (2000) as I report that one does not have to look very hard to find social problems *even in Sweden.* The questions of skeptics and Pred's use of the word "even" imply that Sweden holds a place in the popular imagination as exceptional. As Pred wrote, the country is "stereotyped by Western intellectuals and progressives as a paradise of social enlightenment, as an international champion of social justice, as the very model of solidarity and equality, as the world's capital of good intentions and civilized behavior toward others" (Pred 2000, 6). Pred argued that the beliefs embedded in this stereotype—moral superiority and intolerance of injustice—are what allow Swedish racism and ethnocentrism to persist.

Stereotypes about Sweden are based on outdated notions of a strong Swedish welfare state and ignore the "slow and deliberate dismantling" of welfare policies over the past forty-five years (Sernhede, Thörn, and Thörn 2016, 157). Neoliberal policy has increasingly shaped urban governance in Sweden since an economic crisis in the 1970s.[3] Economic crisis in the 1970s led social democratic leaders to seek out market-based solutions, and welfare retrenchment led by a center-right government began in earnest during a national financial crisis in the early 1990s (see Chapter 2 for full discussion). In 1991 the government abolished the Ministry of Housing and introduced measures to privatize public housing (Andersson and Turner 2014; Christophers 2013; Hedin et al. 2012; Sernhede, Thörn, and Thörn 2016).

These changes in housing policy were critical for two reasons: first, this was a pivotal moment in welfare retrenchment. Affordable housing had been "a pillar of the Swedish democratic welfare state, catering as it did to basic needs of the broad working and middle classes," but when Social Democrats came back into power in 1994,

---

3. Analyses of the extent to which neoliberalism has taken hold in Sweden vary among social scientists working in Sweden (see, e.g., Christophers 2013 and Franzén, Hertting, and Thörn, 2017).

they did not reconstruct pre-1991 housing policy (Hedin et al 2012, 444). Second, in the absence of support from the state, cities become entrepreneurial to find new sources of funding (Lauermann 2018). Changes in housing policy allowed for tenure conversion—the shift from rental properties to cooperative market-based housing. In addition to spurring competition among middle- and upper-class buyers, it also contributed to deepening class segregation in Sweden's major cities (Thörn and Thörn 2017). The combination of welfare retrenchment and increasingly competitive housing markets paved the way for gentrification in Sweden's city centers.

Sweden's Major Cities

Like many cities around the globe, Sweden's three major cities (Stockholm, Göteborg, and Malmö) followed a trajectory of deindustrialization. Each city is home to similar post-industrial neighborhoods: Södermalm in Stockholm, Haga in Göteborg, and Möllevången in Malmö. As I discuss in Chapter 3, these neighborhoods hold significant symbolic power for urban autonomous movements. They were all working-class industrial centers and labor movement strongholds that transformed to gentrified centers for an upwardly mobile middle class. However, this process happened at different rates and in different decades, making a comparison of the three useful for understanding change over time. Gentrification began in Södermalm in the 1970s, urban activists battled to "save Haga" in the 1980s, and Möllevången began seeing indications of gentrification in the early 2000s. To urban social movement actors, this not only means that they are pushed out of city centers but also represents a symbolic erasure of the labor movement gains that came before them.

Malmö, where I begin this book, is Sweden's third-largest city with a population of approximately 340,000 residents (Malmö Stad 2019). Part of Denmark until the mid-seventeenth century, Malmö became an important port in northern Europe in the 1850s and home to major textile industries around the turn of the twentieth century. Owing to its history as a major industrial center, Malmö is home to the robust Swedish labor movement. An economic recession in the mid-1970s hurt the manufacturing industry in the city, and a decade later, the Kockums shipyard—one of the largest in Europe—closed,

Kiruna
Kebnekaise
FIN.
Norwegian Sea
Arctic Circle
Luleå
Skellefteå
NORWAY
Umeå
Gulf of Bothnia
Sundsvall
FINLAND
Gävle
ÅLAND ISLANDS (FINLAND)
Uppsala
Norrtalje
Karlstad
Västerås
Örebro
Eskilstuna
★ STOCKHOLM
Norrköping
Linköping
Oxelösund
Stenungsund
Göteborg
Jönköping
Borås
Gotland
Kattegat
Halmstad
Kalmar
Öland
Baltic Sea
LAT.
Helsingborg
Karlshamn
Kristianstad
EST.
Malmö
Trelleborg
LITH.
DEN.
Bornholm (DEN.)
0   50   100 km
0   50   100 mi
RUS.

marking the beginnings of industrial decline in the city. In the mid- to late 1990s, the city began to revamp its image as a center of creativity and knowledge, due in part to the opening of Malmö University in 1998. Today Malmö markets itself as a creative, eco-friendly city, sometimes branding itself as part of the cross-border Øresund region with Copenhagen, Denmark (Falkheimer 2016).

Located on the east coast, Stockholm is Sweden's largest city and capital, with a population of more than 960,000 (Stockholms Stad 2020). The city is situated on fourteen islands where Lake Mälaren meets the Baltic Sea and consists of three major areas: the city center, south Stockholm, and west Stockholm. The city center is made up of four major boroughs, including Södermalm ("Söder"), the southernmost borough. Söder was an industrial and working-class borough from the late nineteenth century until the 1970s, when rent regulations changed and industry declined (Franzén 2005). As is the case in many Swedish cities, neighborhoods are class-bound. The closer one lives to the *centrum* or city center, the wealthier one is likely to be. As one moves farther away from the city center, the socioeconomic and occupational statuses of residents drop, precisely the opposite of many American cities (Popenoe 2001). After putting up a fight for territory in Södermalm in the 1970s and '80s, urban movements have also followed this pattern, moving into the southern suburbs as rents in Söder increased and space became less available.

Göteborg is Sweden's second-largest city, with a population of approximately 500,000. The city has a long history of trade and shipping, beginning with the East India Company in the early eighteenth century. As a result, the city was once home to a large shipbuilding industry, until the 1980s when it went into decline. Today, automobile manufacturing is an important industry in the city, and Volvo is the city's largest employer. Though trade union activity is widespread throughout Sweden, there is a long history of labor movement activity in Göteborg, which has long depended on manufacturing jobs to drive its economy. Like Möllevången/Malmö and Södermalm/Stockholm, Haga was an important place to urban social movements in Göteborg's past. A labor movement stronghold in the 1920s, the neighborhood followed a familiar decline alongside

FACING PAGE: **Figure 1.1** Map of Sweden (Credit: University of Texas Libraries)

industrial decline and was slated for demolition in the 1960s. Urban movements emerged to "save Haga," which they did by reversing
Haga's reputation from a slum to a place imbued with historical value
(H. Thörn 2012b).
Gentrification in all three cities was primarily framed by activists in terms of social class, not ethnicity. This might seem especially
surprising in Möllevången/Malmö given the multiethnic character
that one observes on the streets of the neighborhood, from the several Middle Eastern and Asian grocery stores that dot the streets, the
plethora of falafel stands, and the accented Swedish of the men working at the farmers' market in Möllevångstorget. Yet activists across
Sweden during this period used anti-capitalist frames aimed at creating a collective working-class identity in order to "organize the
neighborhood" (Jämte, Lundstedt, and Wennerhag 2020). Activists
in all cities were also responding to visible changes in the neighborhood: new builds, changes in housing tenure, rising rents, and new
amenities geared toward middle-class clientele. Though in Göteborg
and Stockholm, gentrification was already a complete process ahead
of large waves of immigration, change was still visibly under way
in Malmö. Statistical data on Möllevången support activist observations. Between the years 2000 and 2018, the population of Möllevången got younger, wealthier, and more educated, and conversion of
rental properties to co-op or individually owned properties doubled.
Yet the population of people with a "foreign background" (*utländsk
bakgrund*)[4] remained steady (Malmö Stad 2000, 2008, 2019). This
may partially explain why Malmö activists chose a class-based framing of gentrification. Some interviewees also suggested that Middle
Eastern, Eastern European, and Asian shop owners were part of the
bourgeoisie, and therefore not part of the working-class frame. Instead, they said, working-class ethnic enclaves were located in the
Rosengård district.[5]

---

4. This is how city statistical reports identify people born outside the Nordic
region.
5. When asked about ethnic segregation, activists pointed to Rosengård, an immigrant enclave on the outer edge of the city where 60 percent of the population
consists of people with a "foreign background." They did not frame gentrification
in Möllevången as increasing ethnic segregation.

Stockholm, Malmö, and Göteborg share neighborhoods with similar industrial histories, labor movement ties, and gentrification patterns. Yet the processes and pace of neighborhood change happened over different periods of time, making comparison a useful tool for understanding how social movement geographies shape and are shaped by gentrification processes in the short and long term. During my fieldwork this was especially true, as autonomous social movements turned attention to "the local" and made visible, territorial claims on urban space.

Notes on Ethnography and Comparative Study

This book draws on fourteen months of ethnographic research in Stockholm, Göteborg, and Malmö, Sweden between 2009 and 2011 (and a follow-up visit in 2016). This was a key period for studying urban movements in Sweden as a squatting wave swept the country and urban action groups were popping up everywhere (see Chapter 5). By 2016, many of the scene locations I studied had closed, had relocated to new spaces, or were embroiled in disputes with municipal authorities or landlords. At the time of this writing, Cyklopen, in the Stockholm suburbs, is the only social center presented in this book that is still active. This is the nature of studying scenes. As sociospatial structures, they are always in flux, striving for temporal reach. Studying them is like capturing a snapshot.

As I detail in the Appendix, I took field notes at locations that drew a cross-section of social movement actors: community meetings, street festivals, public parks, building sites, and scene locations (bookstores, squats, etc.). I supplemented these observations with formal interviews of thirty-eight autonomous movement actors (twenty-six men, twelve women) and informal conversations with many more. Activists ranged in age from eighteen to thirty-six, with most in their late twenties and early thirties, and for most, working in scene places were full-time jobs. I also conducted textual analyses of archival materials and newspapers in Göteborg in 2010 and Stockholm in 2016 as well as hundreds of pieces of activist media and ephemera.

Given the comparative nature of my research, my field notes reflect a phased approach (Maxwell 2012) to comparative case study. I initially intended to study scenes in Stockholm and Göteborg, but my research in those two cities led me to Malmö. Therefore, this research unfolded in phases, beginning with longer case studies of scenes in Stockholm and Göteborg and followed by multiple short periods of fieldwork in Malmö. The phased approach allowed me to refine my theoretical understandings of scenes as I moved from one place to another. This approach was also practical since the scenes in Stockholm and Göteborg were more difficult to find and the scene in Malmö was so vibrant and easily accessible.

The combination of ethnographic methods and comparative study of three sites is ideal for understanding the interplay of culture and political economy. Interviews and ethnographic observations combined to capture social dynamics of scenes that might not be evident otherwise. For instance, in interviews about the social center Cyklopen in greater Stockholm, people often cited that it was "the most gender equitable building site in history." However, I noticed that most of the activists representing Cyklopen in public meetings were men. When I asked interviewees about this, I learned that the group had suffered schisms along gender lines that had fractured the group. I began asking this question in other places and found that social centers were highly masculine spaces despite their expressed commitments to gender equality and feminist politics. In Malmö, the social center Utkanten held "woman-separatist" Thursdays to encourage women's participation in the space. These examples revealed how activists made sense of inequalities within spaces that prided themselves on egalitarianism.

Comparative study of three different cities reveals not only the variety of ways in which social movement scenes are spatially organized but also some of the driving factors behind why scenes thrive or fizzle. For example, had I only studied Stockholm or Göteborg, we might not understand how social movement scenes can thrive in gentrifying neighborhoods. The narratives in the larger cities were that gentrification equals the death of urban movements. This is not completely untrue, as gentrification does appear to portend an *eventual* end to urban movement scenes. But the Malmö scene also shows us that, at various stages of the gentrification process, urban movements can create opportunities for neighborhood residents to claim space (both physical and discursive); use creative tactics to include as many residents as possible in conversations about the future of their neighborhood; and diffuse the practices of the scene to a wide variety of people. This holds promise for creating more participatory forms of urban development and for slowing the processes of gentrification. In the words of the ever-eloquent David Harvey (2012), "we do not have to wait upon the grand revolution to constitute [democratic] spaces" (xiv).

Road Map: Organization of the Book

Chapter 2 offers an overview of Swedish political culture and social movement histories to situate autonomous movements in national and historical contexts. I trace the history of Swedish urban movements from their roots in neighborhood movements (*byalagsrörelser*) of the 1960s, aimed at preserving historic buildings, through their transformation into more confrontational movements associated with squatting, black blocs, and anarchism. Swedish autonomists challenge nationally accepted approaches to culture and politics by rejecting representative democracy and voluntary association membership, the cornerstones of Swedish political culture.

Chapter 3 looks at how social centers—often the cultural hubs of scenes—are both prefigurative spaces where people imagine a future society *and* spaces in which people seek to preserve the past. Social centers are prefigurative places where people are encouraged to make their own rules. This contrasts greatly with the formal, bureaucratic processes that characterize Swedish political culture. Represented by the unofficial squatters' slogan "Sweden Ends Here," activists seek to distance themselves from notions of "Swedishness" that emphasize order, bureaucracy, and conformity. At the same time, activists draw on the traditions of an Old Left that is distinctly Swedish as they build social centers. Labor movements of the late nineteenth century created libraries, cultural centers, educational institutions, theaters, and parks to serve the cultural, educational, and recreational needs of workers. This is a culture that contemporary activists admire, and they attempt to re-create a similar style of movement culture—albeit one infused with contemporary political issues and a punk rock aesthetic.

In Chapters 4 and 5, I look at the relationship between scenes and city space to consider how scenes become embedded as part of everyday life (as in Malmö) or fail to become part of the fabric of urban neighborhoods (as in Göteborg and Stockholm). In Chapter 4, I show how the right to the city is used as a vehicle for diffusing autonomous movement culture into a neighborhood more generally. The rights to *appropriation* of space and *participation* in decision-making processes about how space is used are enacted through the projects and places of the scene in Malmö. This, in turn, reinforces the scene by strengthening bonds between people and spurring development of more autonomous places. These actions are partially enabled by the fact that Möllevången, the neighborhood in which they operate, is structurally conducive to the development of a social movement scene. The neighborhood is centrally located, making activism visible, and nationally recognized as a hub of cultural and political activity. The neighborhood remains relatively affordable and accessible to activists, artists, and students (for the time being). There is a constellation of places that are in close proximity to one another, allowing for routine social interactions. Taken together, these attributes and efforts create a sense of durability for the scene in Malmö. Activists' efforts are limited in some ways, such as social control by landlords and city authorities; rising rents in the neighborhood that make accessing space difficult or impossible; and competing notions of what constitutes politics, culture, and protest. However—for the time being—the scene gives autonomous practices a visible, everyday presence in the lives of Malmö residents.

In Chapter 5, I turn to Stockholm and Göteborg to consider what happens when scenes are not as central, concentrated, or visible. In the two larger cities, there are similar social movements as those in Malmö, but different social movement *scenes*. Scenes in Stockholm and Göteborg coalesce around temporary spaces in suburban areas, which gives them a more fleeting character. These cases highlight the importance of physical space for bringing people together. In Stockholm, a lack of centrality, visibility, and concentration of places contributes to the lack of a sense of connection and community among activists. In Göteborg, scene places are concentrated, but they are difficult to find. Although some factors make Malmö structurally conducive to the development of scenes, that is not the case in Stockholm and Göteborg. Social movements in the larger cities operate primarily in temporary spaces, which influences how activists see the future. Because they view places as lending durability and stability to a movement, they do not see temporary spaces as having future reach, thereby limiting their impact on social change. The concluding chapter ties the book's arguments together to consider how social movements are shaped by urban development and effect change in the urban landscape, and how scenes bring vitality and momentum to movements. I reflect on the interplay of structure and agency to consider how the spatial aspects of social movements shape activists' visions for the future. *Making a Scene* encourages scholars to think critically about spatiality in the sociology of social movements and the role of social movements as important actors in urban development.

2

Uniquely Swedish

From Social Democracy to Autonomy

his chapter offers an overview of Swedish political culture and
social movement histories to situate autonomous movements
in national and historical contexts. I trace the history of autonomous movements from their roots in neighborhood movements
of the 1960s, aimed at preserving historic buildings, through their
transformation into more confrontational movements associated with
squatting, black blocs, and anarchism. From the party's inception in
1889, Swedish Social Democrats (the architects of the welfare state)
promoted a national identity based on ideas of collectivity, equality,
and homogeneity. Today, the sense of a common national identity is
being displaced by individualism, difference, heterogeneity, and political and economic internationalism. Autonomists are among the
loudest voices challenging problems resulting from these changes, but
they do so using methods that are *not* traditionally Swedish. Swedish
autonomists challenge nationally accepted approaches to culture and
politics by rejecting representative democracy and voluntary association membership, the cornerstones of Swedish political culture.

Swedish Political Culture

Sweden prides itself on the efficiency of its modern, bureaucratic institutions and long history of voluntary organization membership

and strong electoral system (Amnå 2006a). Autonomists work *outside* the channels of representative democracy and *reject* hierarchical organizations. Although Swedish political actors traditionally favor consensus over conflict, autonomists take to the streets and confront authorities, often violently. In short, Swedish autonomists eschew traditional approaches to culture and politics.

In both European and American studies of Swedish society and political culture, sociologists generally put the welfare state at the center. The Swedish state, with its emphasis on "social citizenship and generous social benefits" in the realms of education, work, healthcare, and family life, has become "a primary example of the social democratic welfare regime" (Olsen 2002, 125). Some examples of policies that are often heralded include high-quality education from preschool through university for all Swedish citizens, up to eighteen months of paid parental leave for all parents, and a high level of women's active participation in government, to name a few. It is not an overstatement to say that many sociologists regard the so-called Swedish Model as *the* most modern, progressive, and egalitarian democracy in the contemporary world (Amnå 2006b; Olsen 2002; Trägårdh 2006).

The fact that many sociologists and political scientists describe the Swedish welfare state as *the* most progressive in the world makes Sweden an interesting place in which to study movements that seek to work outside the boundaries of representative democracy. In countries known for "massive systems of representative democracy and majority rule," extraparliamentary movements challenge "what is normally understood as political" by rebuking these processes (Katsiaficas 2006, 6). This is especially true in Sweden, where political involvement is viewed by both the public and social scientists primarily in terms of party politics and there is a rich history of voluntary association involvement.

For many years, "Swedish politics was based on the assumption that social change could be accomplished through a specific political and administrative process" (Lindvall and Rothstein 2006, 49). Debates on the meaning of "civil society" in the Swedish context are revealing in terms of how political involvement is measured. Swedish social scientists lament that, since the late 1980s, the Swedish public has become increasingly politically disengaged. They contend that these changes are being influenced from two directions: (1) "from above, by the growing fossilization of political parties and popular mass movements no longer able to capture and utilize the political potential of the public," and (2) "from below, by the average Swede's increasingly emaciated interest in direct political involvement" (Grassman and Svedberg 2006, 147). What this demonstrates is that Swedish social scientists tend to measure political participation in terms of political party activity, volunteer organization membership (or voluntary associations, as they are called in Sweden), and individual motivation.

Some Swedish social scientists acknowledge that perhaps political participation or interest is not lacking but simply that some Swedes define what is "political" in new ways (Amnå 2006b; Grassman and Svedberg 2006; Sörbom 2005). Swedish sociologist Adrienne Sörbom (2005, 19) points out:

> The traditional political sociologists' focus (like much political science research) on the parliamentary system cannot explain the trend of an increased engagement outside the traditional political arenas that happen simultaneously with decreased participation in political parties. In order to do that, researchers must look at activities outside the parliamentary system.

To accurately capture political involvement in contemporary Sweden, scholars must look more closely at how people are actually engaging with contemporary social and political issues rather than relying on traditional categories of analysis. Studying social movements in terms of scenes is one way that social movement scholars can move beyond the confines of traditional sociopolitical institutions to examine contemporary forms of social action and the meanings that people give to social and political involvement.

Uniquely Swedish: Folk Movements and the Welfare State

While this book is about contemporary movements, the historical relationships between social movements and the Swedish welfare state are important for several reasons. First, the unique characteristics of early "people's movements" (*folkrörelser*), as they are called in Sweden, explain why Swedish political culture has developed in a way that is uniquely Scandinavian. Second, the welfare state is inextricably connected to Swedish national identity. Third, popular movements actively participated in creating the welfare state with the Social Democratic Party in the 1930s. As a result, the concept of "civil society" as separate from the state is a relatively new idea (Trägårdh 2006; Edling 2019). Therefore, people who participate in autonomous movements "defy the Swedish civil society tradition of being tightly connected with the nation state" (Amnå 2006b, 588).

People's movements were instrumental in creating Sweden's social democratic welfare state, a process that created the mold for, and continues to shape, Swedish political culture. The terms "people's movements" and "folk movements" generally refer to three movements with roots in the nineteenth century: temperance, religious revivalist or "free church," and labor. These movements and the voluntary associations that sprang from them "comprise a national treasure" in the Swedish imagination (Amnå 2006a, 166). The legacy of the people's movements, particularly a strong labor movement, has given Sweden a reputation as "a land of popular mass movements" and a nation of politically active citizens (Grassman and Svedberg 2006, 133).

During the late nineteenth and early twentieth centuries, the "most important collective actor" in most European countries was the working class (Gundelach 1990, 338). In the mid- to late nineteenth century, the temperance[1] and religious revivalist movements began to challenge the authority of the monarchy, the military, and the Lutheran state church. It was within the temperance and "free church" movements that "the idea of social insurance began to grow and gain a foothold in local communities" (Olsen 2002, 128). Both of these movements "supplied the labor movement with many cadres who brought with them the culture of popular movement into the trade unions—in particular the experience of organizing, educating, and

---

1. In its earliest days, the temperance movement was "closely allied with the state church" but underwent a process of secularization that "transformed [it] into a popular cultural movement without religious anchorage" (Bengtsson 1938, 137).

transforming people and changing their lives and living conditions" (Hajighasemi 2004, 94). The Swedish Trade Union Confederation (Landsorganisationen i Sverige, abbreviated LO) was established in 1898. Since its establishment, LO "has had strong links to the Social Democratic Party" (Landsorganisationen i Sverige 2007, 13), giving it "an influential role in shaping government policy" (Agius 2006, 589). Anarcho-syndicalism gathered strength in the labor movement shortly after LO was established. In the summer of 2016, I spent beautiful sunny days poring over microfilm of the anarchist newspaper *Brand* in the basement of the National Library of Sweden. Established in 1898, it is the longest-running anarchist publication in the world and still important to anarchist and autonomous movements in Sweden. The pages of *Brand* in the late nineteenth and twentieth century clearly illustrate that the early years of the labor movement, Marxism, social democracy, and anarcho-syndicalism all played a role in the formation of formal and informal labor organizations. The Ungsocialisterna (Young Socialists), the youth group that published *Brand*, founded the anarcho-syndicalist trade union Sveriges Arbetares Centralorganisation (SAC) in 1910. The group reached its highest membership in the 1920s and 1930s, making it competitive with LO, but declining membership reduced its prominence. Although small and alternative, SAC still exists today and is an important collective actor in the radical left milieu (Jämte, Lundstedt, and Wennerhag, 2020).

Under these historical conditions, the Social Democrats were able to use the labor movement to their advantage in creating the welfare state in the 1930s. The vision of the early *sossar* (Social Democrats) was that Social Democracy was "capable of unifying all the 'little people,' including workers, peasants, and the middle class" (Hajighasemi 2004, 97). They envisioned a strong state that created a political culture in which "wide political majorities and the support of interest groups were thought to be of great value" (Lindvall and Rothstein 2006, 49). The Social Democrats filled dual roles as "the party of the state" as well as "the voice of the people's movements." They were successful in bringing together a cross-class alliance of people, which allowed them to dominate Swedish politics from 1933 to 2006. This created a brand of statism with a strong state on one hand and "emancipated and autonomous individuals" on the other, thereby linking "social equality, national solidarity, and individual autonomy" (Trägårdh 2006, 29). Swedish national identity is inextricably connected to the welfare state. There appears to be a debate among historians about the relative importance of the concept of *folkhemmet* (the people's home). *Folkhemmet* envisions government "as a home that protects the nation's people as much as a family's home protects each of its members" (Agius 2006, 588). Central to the notion of *folkhemmet* are "feelings and values of safety, solidarity and equality as well as homogeneity, similarity, localism and even provincialism" (Amnå 2006b, 588). Some scholars argue that the welfare state is more than a set of institutions, it is the realization of *folkhemmet*. The people's home is part of a "national narrative that has cast the Swedes as intrinsically democratic and freedom-loving, as having 'democracy in the blood' as the Social Democrats put it in the 1920s and 1930s" (Trägårdh 2006, 27). Others dispute this claim, arguing that "it has been repeatedly and erroneously argued that the Social Democrats labeled their program *folkhemspolitik* and that *folkhemmet*, 'the people's home,' constituted their core concept" (Edling 2019, 82). Instead, argues historian Niels Edling (2019), the concept became relevant during economic crisis in the 1990s. He argues that *folkhemmet* was wielded by left-wing political parties as a useful rhetorical tool as part of "a boom for social democratic nostalgia" and criticisms of neoliberalism (Edling 2019, 106). This last point was clearly evident in my interviews with urban social movement actors (see Chapter 3).

All of this set the stage for a very different relationship between "the people" and "the state" than we commonly see in Western Europe or the United States (Agius 2006; Gundelach 1990; Trägårdh 2006). In Sweden, there was not "a clear separation between state and society," as there was in other European countries (Agius 2006, 588). State and civil society were not conceptualized as separate spheres. In the 1950s, for example, the word "state" was replaced with "society" (*samhället*) in Social Democratic leaflets and the terms were used interchangeably through the 1980s (Edling 2019). During this period, the ruling Social Democratic Party wrote about comfort, resources, and security while rarely, if ever, using the word "state." This can be attributed to weak conceptual distinctions that were strengthened in the 1990s with the advent of the term "civil society" but could also be interpreted as tactical "where the nicer and softer 'society' replaced the colder 'state'" (Edling 2019, 88). Swedish political culture developed in a unique way:

> Instead of seeing "civil society" as the crucial repository of freedom and protection against the power of the state, the state was seen as having a legitimate and decisive role to play in eradicating inequalities. (Trägårdh 2006, 29)

Early social movements (in the form of voluntary associations) were in a friendly alliance with the social democratic welfare state from its inception. As a result, even Swedes who believe in a strong state tended to "celebrate the tradition of social movements as well as the longstanding practice of inviting and involving organizations in the long process of turning a proposal into a law or policy" (Trägårdh 2006, 31). These voluntary associations do *not* have an oppositional relationship to the government, but have traditionally partnered *with* the government. This is important because, as I will argue later, the institutional/autonomous divide is what defines contemporary autonomous movements, making Swedish activists' defiance of tradition significant.

Social Movement Shifts

From New Social Movements to Autonomy

In Sweden, as in many other countries, the 1960s brought a shift in the organizational forms of social movements (H. Thörn 1999; Peterson, Thörn, and Wahlström 2018). The people's movements of the nineteenth and early twentieth centuries were organized around formal voluntary associations (Gundelach 1990; H. Thörn 1999; Trägårdh 2006; Vandenberg 2006), such as those that ran *Brand* in its early years. Members of these associations often demonstrated "life-long individual political commitments" by taking leadership roles in organizations and/or structuring their social lives around them, making social movement membership "an essential part of defining individual identity" (H. Thörn 1999, 453). However, the so-called new social movements of the 1960s (e.g., the environmental, women's, peace, and student movements) embraced a shift toward increasingly fragmented, part-time, temporary participation in social movement networks (Della Porta and Diani 2006; Melucci 1996; Micheletti 1995; H. Thörn 1999).

In the early 1970s, a series of "neighborhood movements"[2] developed in cities as offshoots of environmental movements. Neighborhood movements were particularly active in Stockholm, as two major areas of the central city, Södermalm and Vasastan, underwent major redevelopment and spurred a series of protest actions. Neighborhood movements were originally organized geographically, with each neighborhood having its own group. The actions of these early groups were aimed at improving the everyday lives of people in the neighborhood, with goals such as building playgrounds for children, upgrading daycare centers, and creating common spaces, like courtyards, for residents in inner-city neighborhoods to "build neighborly activities among residents" (Stahre 1999, 73). Neighborhood groups became increasingly politicized in the early 1970s, and their organizational form is one that urban action groups still use today: "large, public meetings and direct democracy as the form of decision-making, no recognized leaders, and community and cooperation in neighborhoods as the overarching ideal" (Stahre 1999, 73). Over time, the concerns of these groups grew from the immediate issues facing neighborhood residents to a series of increasingly fragmented and politicized action groups—which were no longer organized geographically but around particular questions—that emphasized anti-commercialism, critiques of urban development, and "striving for community and cooperation" (Stahre 1999, 183).

The anarchism of the early 1980s spread out in towns and cities across Sweden as young people took inspiration from punk rock music and anarchist movements in Europe and the U.K. Swedish anarchism took on a more moderate, sporadic character than its Danish, German, and Dutch counterparts—a character that persists today (Jämte and Sörbom 2016; Thörn 2013). In 1983, the syndicalist

---

2. In Swedish, these movements are called *byalagsrörelser*. The translation "neighborhood movements" comes from Ulf Stahre's (1999) comprehensive history of these movements in Stockholm.

newspaper *Arbetaren* (*The Worker*) declared that "Anarchism Lives." In September 1983, activists in Stockholm convened at an anarchist conference at the Black Moon, a bookshop and café in Södermalm. It was the first anarchist gathering in the city since 1979. The description of this gathering paints a picture of the movement that reflects autonomous movement characteristics today: "A music group from Malung, a newspaper in Karlshamn, libertarian youth in Lindesberg, a printing cooperative in Stockholm, non-violence groups. The new anarchism is a broad movement and it exists everywhere. Now it is gathering" (Hallstan 1983, 3). It found its home in music and writing groups, workers' collectives, activist groups, and youth culture. Many activists of this time were involved in peace movements and anti-nuclear movements that were popular throughout Europe at the time. One of the organizers of the event points out that what these seemingly disparate groups have in common is that they "are social outsiders" and "it's important that one connects with everyone who works on activities that are a bit 'outside' of the social norms" (quoted in Hallstan 1983, 4). The gathering resulted in a contact list of anarchist activists from around the country, designed to promote contact among Swedish anarchists.

In the late 1980s the anarchist movement took on a more radical and militant character with the influx of a younger generation of activists. These young activists were influenced by a politicized punk scene and the "diffusion of political ideas and repertoires of action" via increasing personal contact with anarchists in Denmark and Germany (Jämte and Sörbom 2016, 107). A 1987 report by the Swedish Security Service (Sweden's national intelligence service) comments that "a new and militant anarchist movement has begun to appear. . . . Youth who were previously active in squatting, etc. have begun actions against the USA" (quoted in Statens Offentliga Utredningar 2002, 91). The report goes on to detail attacks against the American embassy in Stockholm, protests in response to an official visit from first lady Nancy Reagan, and attacks on McDonald's restaurants and Shell gas stations as expressions of anti-American sentiments. Anarchist activists of this time created an infrastructure of squatted houses from which a scene emerged. The scene retained an anarchist core but spawned a host of offshoot movements including "radical and anarcha-feminists, social ecologists, animal rights activists and anarcho-syndicalists, as well as other strands of radical left-libertarian activists." (Jämte and Sörbom 2016, 106–107). This transformation of the scene gave the movement a character that was like other European movements of the time. Autonomous movements of the 1990s were characterized by an increased interest in anti-fascism and militancy. In the late 1980s, confrontations between left- and right-wing groups escalated, leading to a desire among anarchist and autonomous activists to organize their networks in more structured ways. In response to annual marches of neo-Nazis and nationalist organizations, the first Anti-fascistisk Aktion (Anti-Fascist Action or AFA) network emerged in Stockholm in 1991. By 1993, AFA was a national network with local anti-fascist groups popping up in cities throughout Sweden; their militant, confrontational orientation was clear from the start (Statens Offentliga Utredningar 2002). Central to their operation was to meet right-wing groups where they emerged. Throughout the 1990s and early 2000s, AFA effectively mapped where right-wing groups operated by reading membership registers and right-wing press, as well as performing reconnaissance of private homes and nationalist gathering places.

The Göteborg Riots (2001)

Several of my interview participants mentioned the Göteborg Riots as a "turning point" for the extraparliamentary left in Sweden. Negative portrayals of autonomous activists as "hoodlums" in the newspapers, violent clashes with police (see Säkerhetspolisen 2009), and long jail sentences for activists involved in the protests contributed to a sense of disillusionment about political institutions among leftist activists (see, e.g., Granström 2002; Wennerhag et al. 2006; and Zackariasson 2006). In turn, this led to increased discussion about the importance of activist-managed places organized around do-it-yourself (DIY) politics, which promote direct action as a means of social change.

The Göteborg Riots negatively influenced activists' attitudes toward social and political institutions whether they participated in the riots themselves or just heard about the experiences of others. The events of 2001 also changed the way some activists thought about

Sweden as a whole; because they had grown up with an idea about Sweden as an ideal democracy, the violence and injustice they saw in the treatment of activists during the riots shattered their perceptions of Sweden as a democratic and peaceful country. In my interviews, the importance of the riots particularly stood out among activists in Göteborg and Malmö. In Göteborg, the riots led some people to leave movements, while others were drawn to Göteborg because of its new image as a radically left-wing city. In Malmö, where the riots weren't quite so close to home, the events surrounding the EU Summit galvanized activists and sparked discussions about self-managed spaces where activists could meet, socialize, and feel safe.

In June 2001, Göteborg hosted the EU Summit, an international meeting of world leaders to discuss economic growth, sustainable development, and the expansion of the European Union (EU). The summit included the first presidential visit from former American president George W. Bush, who was there to discuss the World Trade Organization (WTO) and issues related to the Middle East with EU leaders. According to government reports, the summit drew roughly 50,000 demonstrators, 2,500 police, and 2,000 media representatives (Statens Offentliga Utredningar 2002).

Drama surrounding the protests began at Hvitfeldtska Gymnasiet, a school. Göteborg's Action, an activist network, was given permission by the city of Göteborg to use the school as a convergence center and residence. At eleven o'clock in the morning on June 14, riot police surrounded and closed off the school. No one was allowed within one block of the school, and no one was allowed to enter or exit the building. None of the 400-plus activists inside knew what was going on. A large crowd gathered outside the police perimeter as well. A standoff between activists and police ensued, with activists demanding that they be allowed to go and join protests and police charging back with horses, batons, and dogs. As a result, some 240 activists were arrested on charges of "violent rioting" and the police received heavy criticism from protesters and other witnesses. The police later said that they had received reports that activists had potential weapons (e.g., cobblestones and baseball bats) inside the school—reports that proved to be unfounded. Protesters at the school saw the police action as a clear provocation. According to them, the police's actions "had no purpose but to scare people away from protesting" (A. Larsson 2001, 35). The police chief said the action was a precautionary measure, without which he "could not guarantee the EU-meeting and police officers' safety" (Nandorf 2001, A6). The events surrounding Hvitfeldtska Gymnasiet set the tone for the rest of the summit protests. Street battles between activists and police occupied news headlines in every major Swedish paper, peaking on June 15. A cobblestone thrown by an activist hit a police officer in the head. In response, police fired on demonstrators, injuring three people. Two demonstrators were shot in their legs and one caught a life-threatening shot to the chest. Later, police were sent to deal with "violent actions" (fights, fires, and thrown cobblestones or bottles) erupting in various parts of the city. People on the streets were reportedly asking journalists how to get home, not knowing how to safely navigate the city. The city hospitals, swamped with injured people, set off an emergency alarm around midnight and called all personnel to report to work.

Few people I met actually *attended* the protests in Göteborg. Nearly everyone I met, however, remarked on how the riots affected leftist movements—for better or worse. Hans, a squatter in Stockholm who was only twelve years old in 2001, remarked that "the left took a real hit during those protests. A lot of people stopped being activists after that." For Hans, the riots negatively affected leftist movements because the police repression they faced during the protests caused some people to leave movements, thereby weakening leftist movements. For Maja, an activist involved in AFA and the asylum rights group No One Is Illegal in Göteborg, it had the opposite effect. She was a child in 2001 but was on Avenyn (the main avenue in Göteborg), where the majority of violent clashes happened between police and activists. She attended with her parents, who are active communists. Though she was not personally involved in rioting, Maja remembered thinking that it was "exciting and fun to be a part of something like that" and she credits the experience with awakening her interest in protest. Maja also claims that the events of 2001 "have made [activists] more paranoid about police," saying that "the cops think that every crime has something to do with us, and I think it's because they think badly about activists ever since 2001."

Maja believes that since the riots, the police view activists as potential criminals, creating caution and suspicion among radical groups about who participates in their spaces. Mattias, also in Göteborg, was one of the few people I met who *was* in attendance at the protests in 2001. He says that the riots contributed to Göteborg's image as a politically radical city, which had both positive and negative effects for the activist community:

> After the riots in 2001, a lot of people wanted to move to Göteborg it felt like, and get involved [in activism], which is both good and bad. It's a lot of people just wanting to get into it because it's a status thing, which is bad . . . but many want to do political things and got interested in it because of [the riots], which is good.

The riots created an image of Göteborg as a city of activists, a radical city, a city where people broke rules—and laws. Mattias comments that the negative effects of this are that people were attracted to activism because it seemed exciting and cool, not because of any underlying political commitment. The positive, though, was that more people became interested in political issues after the riots.

It has been well established by Swedish social scientists that the riots changed the way that left-wing Swedish activists view political institutions and democracy. Psychologist Kjell Granström (2002) found that after the riots, activists' beliefs in politicians, police, the mass media, and the rights of demonstrators decreased as a result of what they saw as unjust actions by those involved in these institutions. As part of an ongoing debate over whether young people in Sweden are politically apathetic or simply engaging in politics in new forms, ethnologist Maria Zackariasson (2006) found that the Göteborg riots were meaningful to people who were involved in the riots as well as people who heard firsthand accounts from other people but were *not* present themselves. She also found a distrust of political institutions, but the activists she interviewed reported feeling even more propelled to action by the events of the riots. The injustices they spotted during the riots led them to want to take action—albeit outside the bounds of institutional politics. A survey of more than a thousand Swedish activists involved in the global justice movement found that 57 percent reported that their belief in the government decreased since the riots and 40 percent reported that they did not believe in political parties at all (Wennerhag et al. 2006). These findings were roughly the same for people who were in Göteborg during the riots and those who were not. The authors acknowledge that many of the people they surveyed did not hold a particularly strong belief in the institutions of representative democracy prior to the riots but that the level of their beliefs still decreased further after the riots.

Following the Göteborg riots, the autonomous left took on a new trajectory (Jämte, Lundstedt, and Wennerhag 2020).[3] Leaving the confrontational militancy of the 1990s behind, a new generation of autonomous activists turned toward local politics of everyday life. Many activists claimed that "the movement had turned into a politically irrelevant subculture" and called for broader changes in school, work, and neighborhoods (Jämte, Lundstedt and Wennerhag 2020, 19). Local politicians and elites became the adversaries, and activists called on a broader swath of people to "organize your neighborhood," taking on questions of privatization, housing, public transportation, and so on, and increasing mobilization around questions related to urban space.

Squatting Waves

In the early 1970s, the Swedish government lifted regulations on rent, making rent negotiable between landlords and tenants. This change made it attractive for landlords to renovate their buildings and seek higher rents. Political strategies aimed at bringing families from the suburbs into cities also made renovations attractive, especially in working-class districts where buildings contained primarily classic "workers' apartments," many of which were just a single room plus a kitchen and toilet. These changes in policy and political strategy laid the groundwork for the gentrification of working-class areas

---

3. Few studies examine the current autonomous left in Sweden (notable exceptions include Polanska 2019; Hansen 2020; Jacobsson and Sörbom 2015; Jämte 2013; Jämte, Lundstedt, and Wennerhag 2020; and Piotrowski and Wennerhag 2015).

such as Södermalm in Stockholm—and protests against it (Franzén 2005).

Squatting was a sporadically popular political tactic throughout the 1970s but picked up steam in the 1980s. Influenced by Danish squatters in the BZ movement, squatting continued to be a popular tactic in Sweden throughout the 1980s and '90s (see, e.g., Polanska 2019 and Pries and Zackari 2016). While squatting in the 1970s was aimed at saving buildings from demolition and renovation, in the 1980s and '90s, squatters drew attention to housing shortages in large cities. In the late 1990s, autonomous movements shifted from conceptualizing the right to the city solely as a critique of housing politics, as it had been in the 1980s, to more philosophical ideas about urban life and neighborly relationships.

In 2007, the Danish social center Ungdomshuset was evicted by city authorities after twenty-five years in its Copenhagen location. Ungdomshuset was a place that many Malmö activists knew intimately, and demands for urban space, particularly in the form of squatting, and debates over who has the right to the city began to emerge throughout Sweden. A 2009 newspaper article from the newspaper *Göteborgs-Posten* proclaims that "a new wave of building occupations is sweeping over Sweden" (Grahn-Hinnfors and Hugo 2009). The article goes on to detail several squatting actions that took place between 2008 and 2009. The goals of the squatting actions were reminiscent of squatting movements in the past. Demands ranged from protests about lack of housing and class segregation (like movements of the 1970s and '80s) to stopping demolitions of buildings to gaining access to space in which to build social centers (like movements of the 1990s).

Because authorities take a zero tolerance approach to squatting, it is still not a viable tactic for procuring housing. Writing for the activist magazine *Brand*, the prominent Stockholm activist Mattias Wåg (2010, 27) writes that "so far it has been a symbolic activist movement." Most squats in Swedish cities do not last for an extended period—often just a few days or a week—making it too unstable as a form of housing. Instead, contemporary Swedish autonomists engage in three kinds of squatting: political, conservational, and entrepreneurial. *Conservational squatting* refers to squatting that aims to preserve buildings or an existing urban landscape (Pruijt 2013). This logic was more often used by earlier generations of squatters, like those inhabiting Mullvaden (Polanska 2019). However, this form of squatting is not only about physical space but also about preserving a particular sense of place, as I discuss in later chapters; activists who take over buildings often do so in the name of preserving the *character* of the neighborhood, not just the buildings.

More often, though, the current generation of squatters use the logics of both *entrepreneurial* and *political squatting*. Entrepreneurial squatting refers to occupying space in order to create a social or cultural establishment. This form of squatting is most central to attempts to create a network of places that form a social movement scene. Political squatting refers to the idea that squatting a building is not the goal in itself (Pruijt 2013); it is a tactic aimed at drawing attention to political issues, such as a lack of housing.

When asked directly, some squatters say that the political goal is to draw attention to a lack of affordable housing. Lena, a squatter and asylum rights activist in Göteborg, says, "A house is something everybody should have. Cultural places, that's something society can always bring out in some way, but a house is something more important because everyone should have somewhere to live." Lena engages in squatting to draw attention to a lack of housing in Göteborg because she believes that having a home is a basic human right, something to which all people should have access.

However, my data suggest that a combination of entrepreneurial and political squatting is most common in Sweden. As Rikard, a squatter in Stockholm, told me, "I think people have the need to have a social meeting place, where they can feel like they're taking a little break from the capitalist world . . . in a place where people don't need to have money to be there, you don't have to buy anything just to be there if you want." Rikard points to the importance of squatting in order to create an environment where the purpose is socializing, not spending money. An issue of the syndicalist magazine *Direkt Aktion* reports that "squatting movements have focused on fighting to create 'autonomous space' . . . and demand to be able to use them or get access to other facilities from property owners in exchange, as self-managed community centers, so-called 'social centers'" (Ingman

2009, 21). In this case, activists squat buildings to draw attention to a lack of available space in cities (political squatting) *and* demand space for social and cultural activities (entrepreneurial).

The Myth of *Folkhemmet* ("The People's Home")

The decline of industrial economy began in the 1970s in Sweden, culminating in severe economic recession in the 1990s. While Sweden maintained low rates of unemployment compared to other Western European countries throughout the 1980s, impending economic crisis forced the Social Democratic government to begin reducing welfare benefits (J. Andersson 2009). Welfare retrenchment in the 1990s "represents a central turnaround in the Swedish national psyche, and political consciousness, as the pride in being the most modern country in the world, and the feeling of embodying modernity was replaced with a sense of disorientation, and loss" (J. Andersson 2009, 238). As a result, people growing up in the 1980s and 1990s faced an uncertain future. Welfare retrenchment of the 1990s represented "a national trauma" that created a period of economic and social instability unparalleled in postwar Sweden (J. Andersson 2009, 238). The promise of *folkhemmet* ("the people's home")—a state that took care of its citizens as if they were a family—began to seem even more unlikely to young people.

People who grew up believing in the ideas of *folkhemmet* found themselves disillusioned when they saw or experienced inequalities in their own communities. This is likely the result of two competing forces: rhetoric about social democratic nostalgia and a widening gap between that vision and the realities. Anarcha-feminist Salka Sandén (2007, 8) writes that in the 1980s,

> we were expected to embrace a picture of ourselves as happy products of a democratic welfare society, when all we saw around us was stagnation, quiet desperation, powerlessness, decaying schools and an adult world that had long ago stopped believing its own words.

Sandén points out the widening gap between the ideals of *folkhemmet* and the realities that she and her peers saw in their own neighborhoods. While the national narrative about Sweden cast its people as "happy products of a democratic welfare society," Sandén (2007, 8) saw "massive unemployment, privatization, surveillance of public space, and individualism." She describes her generation as one caught between two systems: a postwar ideal that emphasized collectivity, common goals, and a secure future and the reality of the 1990s, which, in her world, included individualism, commercialization, and uncertain futures.

Jenny, who has been involved in squatting movements in both Malmö and Stockholm, points out how growing up in the 1980s and '90s shaped her views of society:

> Many of us who are part of the squatting movement now were raised in the '80s and '90s and the whole time we were growing up . . . the welfare that had always existed [in Sweden] was being cut back. We have learned that one cannot trust that one is going to get anything because there isn't anyone looking out for us. One must either struggle individually or go and stir things up collectively.

Jenny's comments also point to the widening gap between the ideas of *folkhemmet*, which stressed the state's role in taking care of its people, and the realities of life in contemporary Sweden where some people feel they can no longer rely on the welfare state to meet their needs.

In the preceding quote, Jenny says that in order to be sure that people get what they need, they must make it happen themselves, collectively. People of her generation, who grew up in the 1980s and '90s, "were confronted with a social reality their parents had never encountered. A generation who grew up in an era of steady welfare expansion was confronted with the end of welfare, or at least, with cutbacks rather than reform" (J. Andersson 2009, 238). This is reflected in the written call to action that preceded a 2010 street party and protest in Stockholm called Take Back the Welfare (Ta Tillbaka Välfärden). Organized by numerous autonomous networks in Stockholm, the manifesto begins, "Welfare was built for a generation with steady employment, with life-long jobs, so that workers could manage temporary slumps in the job market. It does not look like that anymore. Our life situations do not look like that" (Ta Tillbaka

Välfärden 2010b; also 2010a). In this statement, activists recognize that economic and social changes have created different living conditions for young people than those their parents faced. Swedish political culture developed in such a way that social movements developed a close working relationship with the state. The welfare state remains integral to Swedish national identity and to scholarship on Swedish politics and culture. Social movements from the 1960s onward have rejected this close relationship between movements and the state. Autonomous movements seek to operate independently of political parties and outside the boundaries of capitalist systems as much as possible. Activists in these movements are bored and frustrated by the lack of action they perceive among lawmakers in formal political institutions. By mobilizing around the right to the city, they seek to operate self-managed spaces in which the practices and relationships of everyday life become politicized immediately.

3

Social Centers

Where Past, Present, and Future Meet

A building can be a whole movement's heart, a central
point where people pulse through and gain power.
(Anarkistiska Studier 2008)

Scenes are prefigurative spaces. Prefigurative politics refers to
the idea that "social change requires creating and experimenting with the kinds of egalitarian practices, democratic spaces,
and alternative modes of relating that anticipate a future society that
cannot yet be fully realized" (Cornish et al. 2016, 115). In other words,
prefigurative politics are rooted in the present and oriented toward
the future. For autonomous activists, the future appears uncertain
and the possibilities for social change are shrinking, given strict rules
and regulations that characterize public life. Scenes, with their connotations of malleability, expansion, and freedom, offer possibilities
for experimentation and change.

Autonomous social centers are vital for urban movements because
they are hubs where people experiment with political perspectives
and social norms, circulate new ideas, and diffuse these ideas to the
broader community (Yates 2014, 2020). Social centers house activities such as political meetings, book and film discussions, parties,
art workshops, and carpentry or building workshops. Some social
centers are purely (counter)cultural spaces; others also serve as living
and working quarters. Social centers are closely linked with squatting movements but are not always squatted spaces (Vasudevan 2017).

Studies of Italian and British social centers show that these spaces can be "collectively owned, rented, squatted, temporary, or more permanent . . . but they all rely on collective and cooperative principles" (Pusey 2010, 178; also Hodkinson and Chatterton 2006; Mudu 2004; and Piazza 2012).

Prefigurative processes take shape in social centers. Sociologist Luke Yates (2014, 2) frames prefiguration as a series of five distinct but related processes: "experimentation, the circulation of political perspectives, the production of new norms and conduct, material consolidation, and diffusion." In prefigurative places, activists experiment with social, cultural, and political practices and perspectives that are in some way "alternative" to the society in which they live. These perspectives are then circulated within the scene via alternative media, discussion groups, protests, and so on. The circulation of these ideas contributes to the production of new norms and values that characterize autonomous places. Norms, codes of conduct, and political symbols become inscribed on the physical environments of these places (how they are organized, built, decorated). Diffusion refers to the transmission of these norms, practices, and ideas both temporally (beyond the present) and spatially (beyond the walls of scene places) (Yates 2014).

Recent social movement scholarship thoroughly interrogates the relationship between the present and the anticipated future (see, e.g., Creasap 2020; Gordon 2018; Swain 2019; and Wagner-Pacifici and Ruggero 2018). Yet my data suggest that Swedish urban movements also draw on the past in the form of social movement histories. In the process of creating social centers—exemplary of the prefigurative processes that Yates (2014) outlines—Swedish activists simultaneously draw on traditions of the Old Left that are distinctly Swedish and distance themselves from notions of "Swedishness" that emphasize engaging in politics and culture via formal institutions and conforming to social norms. While rejecting institutions and conformity may be common in other European autonomous movements, my interviewees explicitly link these dimensions of autonomy to Swedish history and culture.

When the Social Democratic labor movement became Sweden's ruling party, the movement's cultural institutions (parks, cultural centers, libraries, etc.) also became formally operated by unions and/ or the state. Since autonomists reject the state as an authoritative body, they also reject many of the cultural institutions of the former labor movement as they exist today. Yet they draw on the practices and values of the twentieth-century labor movement, which also prioritized building self-managed places free from state control. As the quote that begins this chapter intimates, social centers are vital locations in the emergence and maintenance of scenes because they are hubs where people experiment with political perspectives and social norms, circulate their ideas, and diffuse these ideas to the places in the scene. I begin this chapter with a description of three social centers, each representing one city (Utkanten/Malmö, Kulturhuset Underjorden/Göteborg, and Cyklopen/Stockholm). I then discuss the "old" (labor movement) and "new" (rejecting "Swedishness") cultural frameworks upon which activists draw in creating, maintaining, and diffusing the practices and norms in scene spaces. Next, I use the processes of prefiguration, elaborated by Yates (2014), as an analytical framework for showing how social centers are hubs for experimenting with politics and culture, circulating ideas, producing new norms, and creating physical spaces imbued with political meaning.

The Social Centers

Social centers are central to autonomous scenes in Europe. In self-managed places people engage in cultural and political projects that are outside the bounds of traditional Swedish politics (i.e., parties and formal organizations). In social centers, activists encourage people to break free from existing political practices and experiment with new ones. In these places, activists prioritize a politics of everyday life with an emphasis on social relations; mundane acts such as washing dishes, showing films, and serving food take on political meaning in these places. These practices draw upon some practices of the early labor movement. At the same time, the do-it-yourself—or, as one activist put it, "do-it-together"—ethos by which these places operate is, for many, a welcome respite from the "stiff" and "controlling" rules and regulations that activists say characterize public life in Swedish cities. These centers are central hubs from which information, practices, and norms circulate throughout the scene. Although social centers promote egalitarianism and social justice, they are not places free from conflict. In Göteborg, a core group of activists worked the social center Underjorden, which made it feel socially "closed" to newcomers and contributed to burnout in those who worked there. This is an example of how a place can come to feel like a clubhouse for activists and their friends that is relatively unopen to outsiders. Gender and ethnicity also operated to convey social power in autonomous spaces—despite their stated goals to the contrary. In both Malmö and Stockholm, gender inequalities arose in social centers, which were predominantly male spaces. In Malmö, the social center Utkanten instituted "women-only" days during which the space was only open to women. In Stockholm, gender inequalities fractured the group who built Cyklopen, creating a divide between those who privileged relationships and those who prioritized building.

At the time of my fieldwork, the groups operating social centers were predominantly white and European, if not entirely Swedish. In Malmö, this particularly stood out to me, as Möllevången is home to several food markets and shops owned by immigrants from Iraq, Afghanistan, and many other places. I came to learn that many of the shopkeepers live in Rosengård—a neighborhood whose name is synonymous with immigrant communities in Malmö. In 2009 Swedish autonomists organized a protest called Reclaim Rosengård aimed at drawing attention to run-down apartment buildings, lowering rents, calling out racism among police, and finding meeting spaces for youth in Rosengård. Reclaim Rosengård stirred tensions among leftists and left-wing groups and Muslim residents in the neighborhood. Mina, a young Muslim woman born in Sweden to Iranian parents, told me that she had always wanted to be involved in leftist politics when she was younger but cited actions like Reclaim Rosengård as an example of a cultural divide between leftist groups and Muslims in Malmö. "They came [to Rosengård] to protest the living conditions there, but it was like they didn't know what they were talking about. I grew up in Rosengård and I am sympathetic to leftist politics, but the way they went about it was all wrong. First of all, they planned a protest during Ramadan. They didn't even know that much!" Newspaper reports claim that Reclaim Rosengård was criticized both by members of the Communist Party, who said the protest was "flippant, counterproductive, and merely aimed to provoke a confrontation with police" (*Sydsvenskan*, August 24, 2009) and by Rosengård locals, who characterized activists as "drunken upper-class kids [who] come here and speak on our behalf" (*The Local*, August 23, 2009). Ethnic and class divides, poor relationships with Rosengård residents, and self-interest got in the way of achieving the goals of the protest. However, the social center Kontrapunkt in Malmö became central to migration activism in Sweden *after* my fieldwork ended, so this may have changed in the intervening years (see Hansen 2019 and 2020 for a rich description of this work in Malmö).

In the wake of violent protests in Göteborg in 2001, many Swedish activists' views on democracy in Sweden were dramatically altered (Wennerhag et al. 2006). For those who grew up during times of increased welfare retrenchment in the 1990s, the events in Göteborg confirmed their notions about how little the welfare state would do for them in the future. Several interviewees said that the negative media portrayal of Göteborg activists and violence in the streets created a need among activists to rebuild a sense of community. In Malmö, Göteborg, and Stockholm, movements aimed at creating social centers—self-managed places used by activists for cultural events, discussion groups, meetings, and community meals—emerged in the early to mid 2000s.[1]

The following sections describe social centers in each city. All three social centers emerged at around the same time (the mid-2000s) and hosted similar kinds of events and activities. Although they were all forced to change locations for various reasons, they still exist in new locations/forms. This highlights the ephemeral qualities of scenes but also demonstrates that the practices of the scene persist,

---

1. During mass protests at the G8 Summit meetings in Genoa, Italy (July 2001), social centers offered information and free meals to activists. Some scholars claim that these experiences inspired people to create social centers everywhere from Australia to the United Kingdom during the early part of the decade. The Swedish case may be another example of this, although activists more often referred to being inspired by the riots in Göteborg in 2001 and the eviction of Ungdomshuset in Copenhagen in 2007.

both temporally and physically, despite hardships and/or changes in locale.

Göteborg: Kulturhuset Underjorden (2006–2011)

To get to Göteborg's social center, Kulturhuset Underjorden (The Underground Culture House), I took a tram over the Götaälv bridge to a neighborhood north of the city center called Gamlestaden (Old Town). As one rides over the bridge, Göteborg's industrial past is on display. The skyline is characterized by ships; massive, colorful cranes; low industrial buildings; and copper rooftops. As the tram travels northeast along the railroad tracks that lead to and from Central Station, it passes rusty rail yards, cement block buildings, dumpsters covered with graffiti, and empty shipping containers.

Underjorden is not easy to find—authenticating the word "underground" in its name and why Lena, an activist in Göteborg, described it as "really cool but at the same time, a mysterious place." I depart the tram in front of a large, brick building with clock towers, a factory that produces ball bearings for the auto industry.[2] Opened in 2006, Underjorden was housed in what used to be the Göteborg Workers' Theater (Figure 3.1). The sign over the doorway is small and difficult to read and the bars over the doors make it appear to be off-limits to passersby. Despite what interviewees described as its "mysterious" locale, the café was familiar to many young people I met in Göteborg who were not involved in activism. Some of them had been to the weekly people's kitchen, not for any political reasons but because it was cheap to eat there. They are familiar with the autonomous politics of the people who run the place. As one cynic said, "Food that cheap must have an ideology behind it."

In 2010, a discrepancy arose between the municipality that owns the building and the activists running the social center. In order to pay their bills—which, according to my interviews, ran nearly three thousand dollars per month for rent and electricity—they allowed bands and activist groups to rent the space from them for shows, parties, and events. In the summer of 2010, the municipality told activists that those practices were not allowed and they would need to

---

2. Svenska Kullagerfabriken (SKF).

Figure 3.1 Entrance to Kulturhuset Underjorden, Göteborg

find a new way to come up with rent money. Alex, who worked at Underjorden, reported that they had been meeting with the municipality to discuss possible compromises: "At the latest meeting they had a nicer tone towards us. But it still feels like they think that, since we don't have money there is no need for our activities and the place should close. We do not agree, it's super important to have free culture" (Nwachukwu 2010). Unable to pay rent or come to an agreement with the municipality, Underjorden closed its doors in 2011.

Stockholm Cyklopen (2007–2008, 2011–Present)

Cyklopen (The Cyclops) was a cultural center located in Högdalen, a suburb on the southern outskirts of Stockholm, from 2007 to 2008 (Figure 3.2). Unlike most social centers in Sweden, it was not rented but built from the ground up by activists themselves. The goal of the project, according to one activist, was to "create a cultural forum

Figure 3.2 Cyklopen, Stockholm (2007–2008). The building was named "The Cyclops" because the single round window above the door resembled the eye of the Greek monster of the same name.

that was not bound by cultural rules in any way. To be more free and flexible, non-bureaucratic." Cyklopen was a do-it-yourself space in the truest sense of the term, built and operated by activists who employed DIY principles in architectural design, the found building materials they used, and the kinds of cultural efforts they promoted. After it was destroyed by fire, editorial writers from Sweden's conservative newspaper, *Svenska Dagbladet*, defended Cyklopen, calling it "a Swedish anomaly of cultural independence" (Radio Sweden 2012). In Sweden, where culture and politics operate within formal, bureaucratic frameworks, Cyklopen represented a radical departure.

The use of available materials and innovative design are part of what made Cyklopen especially unique in Sweden, where buildings are ultra-standard. Two shipping containers stacked on top of one another formed the sides of the building. During the beginning of the building period, activists slept on mats inside the containers. Erik recalls that "every night someone, preferably two or three people, would sleep at the site. I remember waking up groggy as hell [and] climbing down the ladder to brew cowboy coffee at the fire pit." The containers served different purposes when the building opened; some were storage spaces, some held workshops and art space. The front door was a drawbridge, which was practical (for loading and unloading large objects, such as band equipment, into the space), functional (it sometimes served as impromptu stage), and theatrical (seeing the entire front of the building open up "was often a dramatic event," according to visitors). The main hall was a performance space where bands could play music. The loft was a lounge area for socializing and discussion group meetings. The open floor plan of the space discouraged privacy, instead encouraging collaboration, collectivity, and sharing among participants. In other words, the physical infrastructure of the building was designed to produce behaviors and norms informed by autonomous politics.

On the night of November 29, 2008, the Högdalen fire department arrived at Cyklopen to find it in flames. Activists gathered at the center, unable to do anything but watch years of hard work burn to the ground. A few days later, arson investigator Christer Söderheim told *Dagens Nyheter*, "We can state that the fire was arson. There is no electricity in the building that could have caused the fire and besides that our investigation shows that the fire started outside the building" (Bergbom and Öjemar 2008). Activists with whom I spoke were adamant that the motivation behind the arson was anti-leftist sentiment, possibly from radical right-wing groups, as the center had been a meeting place for anti-fascists. These suspicions have never been substantiated and the arson remains unsolved. During my fieldwork, an autonomous collective called called Kulturkampanjen was actively recruiting builders and looking for ideas about how their new social center—Cyklopen 2.0—should look. In 2011, building began on Cyklopen 2.0, the next generation of the social center. Funds poured in from supporters throughout Europe to help create the new building, which sits on a lot not far from the site of the original Cyklopen. The social center opened in its new location in September 2013, sparking a new flurry of autonomous activity in the southern suburbs of Stockholm.

Malmö: Utkanten (2008–2011)

My introduction to the Malmö scene came on a cold, rainy day in June 2010. I was scheduled to meet Hans, an anarchist activist who was to be my guide for the day, at a bus stop. I stood shivering inside

Pressbyrån, the ubiquitous Swedish convenience store chain that smells of cinnamon buns and coffee. Hans greeted me with a smile and a hug and we walked together to the autonomous social center Utkanten—one of several projects in which Hans was involved.[3] We walked together for ten to fifteen minutes, and along the way I asked him to tell me about the area of the city we were in. He said it was "a residential area and traditionally working-class neighborhood where workers from a sock factory used to live," referring to Malmö's former textile industry.

The neighborhood is characterized by the kind of solid, blocky buildings that one commonly sees in former working-class districts in Sweden—concrete, heavy, and drably colored in shades of goldenrod, olive green, and brown brick. Hans told me that soon we would cross into an industrial area where Utkanten is located, at the corner of the aptly named Industrigatan (Industry Street). He explained that Utkanten began as a place called Aktivitetshus (The Activity House) but changed its name and moved to this location in February 2008. The landscape on Industrigatan changed dramatically and we passed into a maze of low, brick warehouses that all look alike and are connected by concrete courtyards. As we entered one of the courtyards, Nils said, "We're here!" and I looked around, confused. There is no sign marking that the warehouse housing Utkanten is different at all, except for the graffiti on the metal double doors to the building (Figure 3.3). "Welcome!" he said, as he flung the doors open for me.

Hans gave me the full tour of Utkanten, an extensive network of rooms spanning two stories. The ground floor included what he described as a "cinema," a large room closed off with a dark, heavy curtain. It was filled with secondhand furniture and a projector that someone had left there and never reclaimed. Hans said they sometimes showed films there, followed by discussions, but mostly people just brought their own movies to watch on a large white sheet that hung on the wall. There was a bike workshop, cluttered with bikes and tools, where a group met once a week to learn how to fix bikes. Bike culture is important to autonomous activists because "reclaim the city" politics includes a call for "car-free" inner cities.

---

3. Utkanten reopened in a new location in 2012, but my observations are from their previous location.

Figure 3.3 Entrance to Utkanten, Industrigatan 20, Malmö

In November 2009, Utkanten was raided by police when its "research department" (hacker group) became the subject of investigation. In a statement to the regional newspaper *Sydsvenskan*, the lead police investigator said that the classification of offenses at Utkanten included breaking alcohol laws, fire hazards and explosive devices, preparation for aggravated theft, and hacking (Palmkvist 2009). Police seized the computers in the upstairs computer room to investigate their contents as well as two key-copying machines, various locks, and lock-picking equipment, which they interpreted as preparation to commit burglary. Representatives from Utkanten denied these claims. Activists were also charged with breaking alcohol laws because police found a substantial quantity of alcohol that they suspected Utkanten was selling illegally. Representatives from Utkanten say it was "backstage beer" for bands who play shows there and that the "explosive devices" seized by police were "legal fireworks" (Palmkvist 2009). When I first visited Utkanten in 2010, activists told me that their lease, which was up in March 2011, would not be renewed by their landlord, a move that they interpreted as an eviction based on their legal troubles.

People's Houses and Social Centers: Self-Management and Freedom from the State

The labor movement of the late nineteenth century created libraries, cultural centers, educational institutions, theaters, and parks to serve the cultural, educational, and recreational needs of workers. This is a culture that contemporary activists admire, and they draw on these histories to create a similar style of movement culture—albeit one infused with contemporary political issues and a punk rock aesthetic. They see the creation of social centers and other places as a means of producing continuity for social movements of the past, present, and (hopefully) future.

Although activists in Sweden do not appear to have used the term "social center" until the past decade, social centers' earliest forbears were built by labor activists in the late nineteenth century. Physical places were of great importance to the early Swedish labor movement because they encountered "resistance from established society" when they tried to rent places for meetings and events (Karlsson 2009, 76). Through connections with other labor movements in Europe, early socialist workers' groups began to discuss the idea of creating their own cultural centers, which they called Folkets Hus (People's Houses).[4] The name was chosen by the Swedes because it denoted that workers had a location that "they built, owned, and managed themselves in a collective fashion" (Ståhl 2005, 21). The first People's House opened in 1890 in the southern city of Kristianstad, and within a few years the idea spread across the nation. Today, there are approximately five hundred People's Houses in Sweden (Folkets Hus och Parker 2020).

Contemporary activists do not see People's Houses as welcoming places because of their ties with the state. Erik, an activist and the

---

4. Despite being associated with Scandinavian labor movements, the term "People's Houses" actually originated in Belgium, where the first People's House (*Volkshuis* in Flemish) was established in 1872 (Karlsson 2009). The burgeoning socialist movement in late-nineteenth-century Sweden had many connections to the Belgian labor movement, which gave them the idea to build a meeting place and cultural center for workers and their families.

lead carpenter in the building of the autonomous social center Cyklopen in Stockholm, says,

> [In Sweden] we have the state owned culture houses, the Folkets Hus, and those places are descendant from the same train of thought [as we have] as far as spaces are concerned. Those were all built by workers' movements that wanted cultural spaces that weren't controlled by the state.

Erik makes a clear connection between People's House movements and contemporary autonomous movements, highlighting self-management and freedom from state control as shared ideological territory.

As the traditions of the labor movement became institutionalized when the Social Democrats took national power, movement places became state institutions. Alex explains that People's Houses "are incorporated into the state bureaucracy, the control of the government, so it's hard to use those spaces to create free spaces or autonomous spaces because they're controlled by the state." People's Houses are examples of how the state creates boundaries on places that were originally intended to be open and managed cooperatively by movements. Viktor explains,

> Everyone who tries to organize an event at a Swedish cultural center, which is communal, will first see some kind of book with rules [about] what you could do or couldn't do. . . . We think it's important for a democratic society to have cultural centers that do *not* stand underneath the state or the municipality structure in any way.

Because People's Houses are state-owned institutions, they come with what activists call "rulebooks" for how they can be used. Autonomous activists not only are against the state's institutionalization of cultural places but promote the idea that a DIY ethic is a more democratic mode of operating such places.

When I asked Rasmus, an activist in Göteborg, about the local People's House, he echoed Viktor's statement, saying, "They have some rules for how you can use the place. Like, you have to be a formal group or association. It's also only certain types of culture that they approve of there, like folk dancing or music. They don't want a bunch of punks hanging around." The rule that only formal groups can use space excludes autonomous groups, which are informal, loosely knit networks. Since People's Houses are a product of folk movements, they promote traditional folk music, dancing, and theater as acceptable cultural events, which contrasts with the often avant-garde, punk rock aesthetics of autonomous movements.

Rasmus's statement that "they don't want a bunch of punks hanging around" refers to how he believes authorities perceive autonomous activists as a ragtag group of punk rock troublemakers, not activists engaged in promoting democratic cultural initiatives. His comments are ironic, given the history of the People's House movement. In a history of People's Houses and Parks, Swedish historian Margareta Ståhl (2005, 82) describes the music that people played during labor movement meetings as "confrontational" for the time period and aimed at convincing listeners to participate in the labor movement struggle and strengthening movement solidarity (see also Pries, Jönsson, and Mitchell 2020). With these insights, it would seem that Old Left activists and the "bunch of punks" to whom Rasmus refers might have more in common than meets the eye.

People's Houses in contemporary Sweden operate primarily as conference centers—in fact, some of their websites (e.g., Malmö Conference Center) refer to them as conference centers, not People's Houses. The Göteborg People's House also functions as a conference center but retains some connections to its past, housing a Social Democratic bookstore and several union-related offices. Activists' critiques of this operation strategy are that People's Houses are now places used primarily by international businesses. In an article that issues a call for more social movement places in Swedish cities, two anarchist writers assert that "folk movement spaces, such as People's Houses, began to be used for consumption-based cultural activities rather early on. . . . This paved the way for the later development in which People's Houses began to be rented out to corporations at market price—or sold completely" (Ariadad and Fleischer 2010, 45). Co-opted first by the state and then by capitalist enterprise, People's Houses, according to activists at social centers, are today primarily convention centers aimed at bringing corporate clients to cities.

Social Centers as Prefigurative Places

Experimentation: "Sweden Is a Very Controlling Society"

Social centers allow people to make their own rules, which activists often contrast with formal, bureaucratic political processes of Swedish governing bodies. Many rules on the use of public places in Swedish cities are made by governing bodies like city and district councils, and activists involved in creating scene places are not entirely immune to dealing with such councils—much to their dismay. Activist places must still meet building code requirements and be free of fire hazards if they want to avoid visits from police. However, decisions about the everyday use of these places are made in public meetings that are open to anyone or on the spot by anyone who wants to use the place. In the city park, there are rules about where people can hang flyers and ride bicycles. In DIY places, on the other hand, "no one can tell you that 'you can't do this or that' . . . you don't need permission" ("Utkanten Guide" 2010). The message of DIY places is that you don't wait for someone to tell you what to do; you make the rules yourself.

The "Utkanten Guide" offers a wealth of information on the ways in which people can experiment in social centers. As part of its principle as a "free space" that anyone can use as they desire, Utkanten was never locked, allowing people to come and go at any time of day or night. The guide includes a floor plan that introduces readers to each room in the building, including details such as what electrical outlets do not work (Figure 3.4). It also invites visitors to plan political and cultural activities: "Maybe you want to plan a political meeting? Play a [music] show? A film festival? Show your art? Have a dance group?" These activities—or any other "cultural, social, or political activities" one can conceive of doing—are fair game at Utkanten. The guide also notes in several places that there is a large public meeting (stormöte) every Saturday at two P.M. During this time, people are welcome to come pitch their idea for activities to a larger group in order to gain support of others.

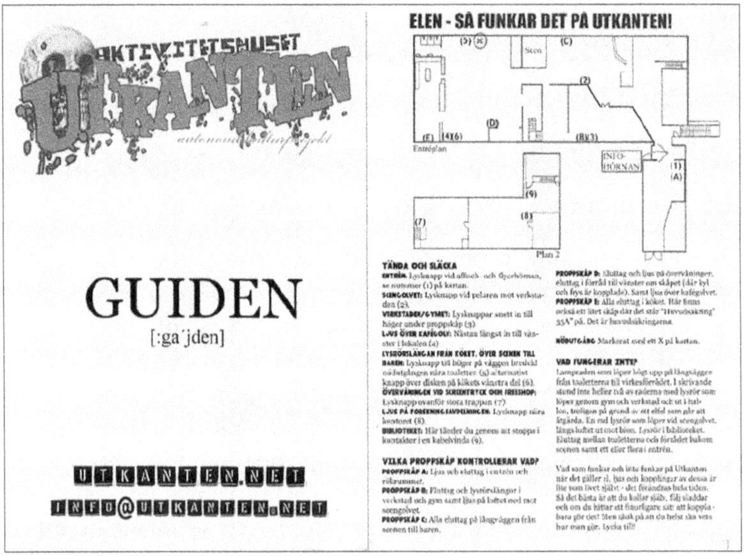

Figure 3.4 "Utkanten Guide," Malmö

In an interview with Milla, who is part of several activist projects in Malmö, she contrasted the ordered, procedural nature of Swedish culture with Spain, where squatted social centers are an established part of activist life:

> Sweden is a very controlling society. If you compare it to, for example, Spain. There is another way of life there, an alternative way of life. You can squat buildings and there is an informal economy, but Sweden is a very controlling society, so it's difficult to be alternative.

Using squatting as an example, Milla explains that pervasive economic and social control gets in the way of people being able to live an "alternative" or countercultural lifestyle.

Rigidity and conformity were common themes when people explained to me why they think leftist scenes break cultural norms in Sweden. I asked Lena, a young anti-fascist in Göteborg, to describe the local social center, Underjorden, and she expressed the idea that it was in some way un-Swedish:

It's like, "Holy shit, do these things exist in Sweden?" [. . .] Sweden is really . . . Sweden is . . . if you describe Sweden as a person, it's a blond, stuck-up person with a stick up his ass. That's Sweden. Too stiff.

Lena expresses incredulity that a place like Underjorden exists in Sweden. For her, Sweden is "too stiff" and conformist. Her description of Sweden as a person highlights the stereotype that all Swedes are alike—blond, stuffy, and snobbish. Underjorden, on the other hand, represents something else, an alternative form of culture where people let loose and can be themselves.

Christof, a young Belgian activist I met in Malmö, said, "In Sweden there is great pressure to conform. Those who dare to reject the social standards seem way out there. I thought Belgium was a conformist society, but I've never seen the same level of conformity [that exists in Sweden] anywhere else in Europe." Because of its history as a homogeneous culture, Sweden, according to Christof, is one of the most conformist societies in Europe. Social centers represent a break from the conformity and rigidity that activists feel characterizes public life in Sweden.

Circulation of Ideas: Graffiti, Activist Media, and Pirate Cinema

In his study of Spanish social centers, Yates (2014, 14) points out that "the organization of seminars, debates, conferences and the production and provision of zines, pamphlets and alternative media encouraged participants to imagine, learn and play with ideological positions." This informs and is informed by cultural and political experimentations. The entrance of Utkanten (Malmö) was decorated with colorful flyers and pamphlets. Hand-drawn announcements about meetings and events hang on the wall over a small shelf of pamphlets about anarchism and flyers from the syndicalist union, SAC. Most of the flyers on the wall announce band performances and/or political meetings at Utkanten.

As at most autonomous places, political symbols cover every available surface at Utkanten as a means of imbuing the place with meaning. The café is furnished with secondhand tables, chairs, and

Figure 3.5 Kitchen at Utkanten, Malmö

couches, and a piano sits in the middle of the room. Brightly colored murals cover the walls and are decidedly political in their themes. On one pillar, a cartoon pig with the word "homophobe" hovering over his head receives a blow to the face from a disembodied fist. On another wall, raised fists of varying sizes—symbols of unity and solidarity—are painted in blue, red, and pink. In the kitchen, a large skull and "crossbones"—made of a knife and fork—is painted on the wall next to the words "Eat the Rich," a clear anti-capitalist message (Figure 3.5).

The discussion groups, film nights, activities, and even mealtimes at social centers are educational experiences. Mia, one of my participants in Göteborg, drew parallels between the educational opportunities in social centers and the labor movement institution of popular education (*folkbildning* or "people's learning"). The cornerstone of *folkbildning* is the study circle in which a group of at least five adult learners choose a topic, read, and discuss ideas (Ståhl 2005). The practices of *folkbildning* were institutionalized in the form of educational centers and schools for adults.[5] Activists see discussion groups that follow films or are organized around books or social issues as forms of popular education. The Workers' Theater that housed Underjorden was attached to a public library, physically linking the labor movement and education.

A popular activity at Underjorden (Göteborg) was the "Pirate Cinema" (Piratbio),[6] a weekly film showing to which admission was free and open to the public. Every Tuesday evening the center would show a film—usually documentaries, often in English—followed by a discussion. On a flyer that listed the film schedule, organizers wrote, "Pirate Cinema Göteborg thinks that Göteborg residents have the right to several free spaces and social meeting places. [At Underjorden] you have the possibility to check out a good film, chat with your friends, and have coffee at a newly opened café all in the same location". Examples of films include *After Stonewall*, which details the history of the LGBT movement in the United States, and *McLibel*, a documentary about a British court case against two environmentalists who published a pamphlet that was critical of McDonald's.

Activists viewed these as both cultural and political events because the films were "more open than 'home theaters' but less anonymous than cinemas and with the possibility to incorporate the film into political discussion" (Ariadad and Fleischer 2010, 46). However, it was not only the framing of films in political discussion that activists considered political about these screenings; they also prioritized these events as ways of meeting new people and "creating a sense of community," which neither home movie screenings nor public cinemas offer: "Pirate movie nights are political not only because they flout copyright laws, but because they create new spaces for film and

---

5. Several adult education centers transitioned from informal study circles to institutions in the twentieth century. The Workers Education Association (ABF) is the one to which activists often refer. I studied Swedish at Studieförbundet Vuxenskolan, which began as a series of informal study circles in the 1920s and were institutionalized as adult education centers in 1967. They are operated independently of the state but are publicly funded. The curriculum is similar to American community colleges (Studieförbundet Vuxenskolan 2014).

6. It was called "Pirate Cinema" because it disobeyed copyright laws by publicly showing films for free.

new possibilities for collectives to gather" (Ariadad and Fleischer 2010, 46). Rather than going to a movie alone or with friends and not speaking to anyone around you, activists prioritized discussions of the film as a means of fostering relationships among people who did not previously know one another.

My observations revealed that informal activities, such as meals, often became educational experiences as well. For example, I attended a "people's kitchen" meal at Underjorden (Göteborg) following a Ship to Gaza protest. The dining area was abuzz with energy that the protest had generated. A few people at my table described themselves as having to "admit" that they really did not understand why or how activists from Sweden were involved in trying to break the blockade on the Gaza Strip. People at the tables around us began chiming in, answering questions and discussing the Free Gaza Movement that Ship to Gaza (a coalition of Scandinavian activists) supports. This informal occasion became a consciousness-raising experience.

"Do's and Don'ts": Production of Norms and Practices

Cultural experimentation, discussions, and debates contribute to "establishing new collective norms, which draw upon both experimental performances and political perspectives or ideas" (Yates 2014, 14). My observations from Utkanten (Malmö) show that norms and practices are established and (re)produced by political signage, literature, and social interactions. In contrast to the drab brick façade of the building outside, the interior walls of Utkanten are covered in colorful graffiti. A jumble of tables and chairs lines one wall, and red paper lanterns hang overhead. Just inside the front door, lists of "do's" and "don'ts" are painted on the wall. The lists reflect the politics of the groups that run the building (Figure 3.6). They read: "DO's: self-initiative, independence, respect, cooperation, solidarity, culture creating without boundaries. DONT's [sic]: racism, sexism, homophobia, heterosexism, violence." The fact that these lists are at the entrance lets visitors know right away what values and norms are agreed upon by people who work and socialize at Utkanten.

The list of "do's" includes the words "independence," "self-initiative," and "creating culture without boundaries." This stands in contrast to the orderly, regulatory characteristics of Swedish society

Figure 3.6 Do's and Don'ts List, Entrance to Utkanten, Malmö

that activists see as confining. Utkanten's Myspace page elaborates on this idea in its description of the social center as an island of autonomy:

> In contrast to the rest of society—where everything is run from above, where we are fed prohibitions, rules, directives and threats of reprisal if we don't obey—we can do what we want [at Utkanten], build activities of our own initiative, work to build relationships with each other in order to counteract oppressive structures.

In this brief paragraph, activists at Utkanten offer a picture of social centers as autonomous oases in a society they feel is characterized by "prohibitions, rules, and directives." In contrast, they describe Utkanten as a place where people can imagine and build activities according to their interests, develop relationships with others, and work together in activism aimed at "oppressive structures," such as sexism, racism, and heterosexism.

An experience that I found quite revealing of the norms at Ut-kanten happened one Monday night as I worked alongside activists in the kitchen in preparation for the weekly People's Kitchen (*folk-kök*). The People's Kitchen, a free weekly dinner open to the public, is a common event at social centers. At Utkanten, all food is procured from the excesses of supermarkets (i.e., taken from dumpsters), a political act aimed at drawing attention to capitalist excess. The group making dinner that evening were an international team consisting of five people; the diners on this particular evening consisted of roughly forty people, including French hitchhikers and a Canadian punk band who shared their beer with me.

Amber, a Canadian student who had been studying in Malmö for a few years, asked what I wanted to make. I replied, "I don't know . . . what are you thinking of making? What do you think will go well with the menu you all have planned?" She said, "It's up to you!" I froze, unable to think of anything to contribute. Being new to the group and an outsider, I was looking for direction from the kitchen crew, who laughed at my indecisiveness. Amber explained my uncertainty by saying, "Sometimes it's hard for people to get used to the concept that this really is a free space. There are no leaders. Just do whatever you feel like." Feeling the pressure of the kitchen crew's smiling eyes staring at me, I said that I didn't have any creative menu ideas, so I would be happy to mindlessly chop and dice vegetables, which I did gladly. Amber and the others quickly incorporated them into a hearty and delicious meal. Having always considered myself an independent thinker, I found it disconcerting that I felt so unsure of how to behave without guidance.

As I washed my coffee cup, I noticed a handwritten sign hanging over the sink. It posed a question: "If you don't wash your own dishes, in practice you like the idea that certain people should live off others' work. Do you know what one calls a person like you in everyday speech?" The question has three possible answers with boxes next to each answer: Bourgeois Asshole, Comrade in Solidarity, or Anarchist. The first possible answer, Bourgeois Asshole, is indicated as correct with a checkmark in the box beside it. This sign is an example of the idea that Utkanten activists promote when they write that one of the norms that they hope to foster is to "build relationships with each other in order to counteract oppressive structures." One of the "oppressive structures" they identify is capitalism. Washing one's own dishes is viewed by activists at Utkanten as an expression of anti-capitalist solidarity in that it shows that one does not expect to live off another person's work. This points to how the meaning ascribed to a place (in this case anti-capitalism) shapes action (washing dishes). The sign points to the politics of everyday life in an effort to make people think about their behavior and inscribe norms for everyday practices that are informed by political beliefs.

Physical Places: "Cyklopen Is Building Future Politics"

Prefiguration[7] includes "attempts to decisively inscribe or consolidate codes of conduct, their political messages and symbolism, and experimental origins" in the physical or built environment (Yates 2014, 14). This may take shape in how people sit during meetings (in circle formations to promote equalizing effects); small libraries containing donated books on social and political issues, reinforcing the educational functions of the social center; and graffiti and printed material (stickers, flyers, pamphlets, zines, and manifestos) from groups such as AFA and Revolutionary Front that cling to the bathroom stalls, walls, and tabletops.

The best example of inscribing places with political meaning is Cyklopen (Stockholm), an autonomous social center built by Kulturkampanjen. For activist-builders there, questions of space and place were intimately connected to their prefigurative strategy. They envisioned themselves as "building the future" by creating a social center. As a physical manifestation of their dreams and imaginations, the building came to serve as an important symbol—locally, nationally, and internationally—of cultural freedom and a hopeful sign for the future of autonomous social movements in Sweden.

Kulturkampanjen is an autonomous collective, and members hold a deep commitment to prefigurative politics. The group perceived that claiming and holding space gave the group *reach* into a long-term future and saw themselves as active agents of change (*volition*) moving

---

7. This section was derived in part from an article published in *Social Movement Studies*, 2020, copyright Taylor & Francis. Available online at https://www.tandfon line.com/doi/full/10.1080/14742837.2020.1798752 (see Creasap 2020).

toward a *contingent* future (or multiple possible futures). These projective orientations influence their actions as a group. For example, Kulturkampanjen fractured as they began to discuss how they could create a gender-equitable building site because the debate revealed disagreement over the future of the group. Were they to focus more on infrastructure and relationships or building their social center? Both were prefigurative strategies designed to experiment with creating gender-equal processes on one hand, and self-managed places on the other. Ultimately, they chose Cyklopen over each other because they perceived that claiming and holding space would have greater *reach*— a temporal extension into an uncertain future. This is just one example of how projectivity plays out in prefigurative social movements.

Since the early 2000s, members of Kulturkampanjen had been squatting for short periods of time in buildings around Stockholm. Tired of being kicked out of building after building, they decided they needed a place of their own. Erik, who was centrally involved in building Cyklopen, explains,

> [Kulturkampanjen] had been squatting and had bad luck with that because of being evicted by cops, but also because of having problems with other squatters. They had been squatting this old metalworking factory or something and they were in there building spaces for cultural activities and other people were in there just wrecking shit and eventually the whole place burned down. So they were kind of exasperated by the squatting scene and were looking for other options.

Erik points out that it was not only police and authorities with whom the Kulturkampanjen were exasperated. He contrasts the members of the group, who were "building spaces for cultural activities," with "other squatters," who were "just wrecking shit." In other words, the members of the group were trying to create something new, while others were being destructive. The exasperation of dealing with places that were temporary, whether due to evictions or clashes between squatters, led the group to seek out other courses of action.

Kulturkampanjen worked with municipal authorities in order to build the original Cyklopen in 2006. As Erik explained, "everything [in Sweden] is really official and above board as far as places are concerned," so cooperation with local authorities was necessary. Focusing on ends (getting land) rather than means (official permission) can be interpreted as capitulation to authorities that undermines broader goals for social change (Halvorsen 2017; Hodkinson and Chatterton 2006). Activists acknowledged this but emphasized that, after squatting multiple buildings over several years and either being removed by authorities or having their work destroyed by vandals, they did not see another path forward. They framed their process as an attack on cultural institutions:

> All movements [in Sweden] . . . must either be incorporated into Social Democracy or totally destroyed. The Swedish government spends lavish resources on cultural development, and has succeeded in keeping public opinion on its side regarding extra-governmental movements. The building of the Cyclops can be seen as a counterattack on this view of culture. (Anonymous 2008, 45)

On one hand, this boldly proclaims that the self-managed, DIY, radical culture of Cyklopen represents a "counterattack" on social democratic institutions. On the other hand, their single-minded focus on building Cyklopen in order to establish longevity is also a form of institutionalization, although it is not state-led.

Evidence of Kulturkampanjen's commitment to reach and longevity also emerged in debates about infrastructure and goals. The group discovered early on that building and technical skills favored men, revealing questions about how to create a gender-equitable building site. A member of Kulturkampanjen penned the following in the anarchist magazine *Rolling Thunder*:

> We realized that our collective skill in building was distributed strictly along gender lines, and we were going to have to engage that problem actively if we wanted to eliminate gender discrimination in our group. That was our intention, and we had a well-thought-out plan that was never completely fulfilled. (Anonymous 2008, 56)

The group's ethical and political commitments to gender equity included modeling gender equity in the building process. Another member of Kulturkampanjen added, "Our general principle has been that every individual shall have the possibility to learn every moment in the building process. If it takes half a day to hammer a nail, so be it" (quoted in Borg 2013). This is a good example of presentist prefiguration; the emphasis is on process in the present, not building quickly. The group planned skill-building workshops and women's separatist work days in order to create a more gender-equal building site. However, none of these panned out.

Deliberation around questions of gender led to a fracture among group members. When I asked why none of their plans for women's workshops actually happened, Karl, a builder on the project, said, "I think some of us prioritized building Cyklopen and others were more concerned with improving relationships with people in the collective." Erik also notes that "schisms and tension" developed in the group because some people "wanted to focus on infrastructure while others of us wanted to focus on our goal." In the end, the group prioritized building:

> Poor follow-through on the part of those who claimed to prioritize relationships within the collective combined with the stubbornness of a goal-focused group led to the collapse of our plans and designs concerning gender equality. . . . The great question that kept reoccuring [sic] in our activities and our debates [was] the central question every group must answer for itself: who are we and what exactly are we trying to accomplish? (Anonymous 2008, 56)

These narratives imply that focus on relationship-building became a distraction, while building the physical structure was the goal. Embedded in this debate is a projective dimension. Activists locate infrastructure and relationships in the present and the building ("the/our goal") in the future. Interviewees acknowledge that the group suffered as a result of this decision, but the longevity of autonomous action more broadly depended on Cyklopen being realized.

The fire that destroyed Cyklopen in 2008 "sent a shock wave through the country's extra-parliamentary left" (Borg 2013). Erik,

Figure 3.7 Cyklopen after the fire, November 2008

who rushed to the scene of the fire, described feeling "an indescrib-able sense of loss. We watched so many years of hard work go up in smoke and there was nothing we could do about it" (Figure 3.7). But activists did not give up. After the shock of the fire wore off, Kulturkampanjen's mantra became "They can never burn down our dreams." When I was in Stockholm in 2009–2010, members of Kulturkampanjen were at every meeting and event I attended to solicit ideas—and builders—for Cyklopen 2.0 (Figure 3.8).

The arson that claimed Cyklopen created a "site of hyper-projectivity" (Mische 2014, 438). Unexpectedly, money and encouragement from people all over Europe rolled in, prompting Kulturkampanjen to roll up their sleeves and begin deliberating about their future. When I met with Mads, one of the organizers of the Anarchist Book Fair in Stockholm, he said, "Hey, if you see anyone from Cyklopen, tell them that I have money for them." He had recently been in Germany, where anarchist groups had collected money to help with rebuilding efforts.

Sometimes support came from unexpected sources. According to Erik, "We received so much verbal support from major cultural institutions like Kulturhus, the Modern Art Museum, politicians—even

Figure 3.8 Flyer: "Do you want to have a free cultural center? Help us build it! Cyklopen needs you." (Credit: Cyklopen)

conservative parties were supportive." Members of national and European parliament—particularly those in left-wing parties—created petitions, wrote about Cyklopen on blogs, and encouraged people to offer financial support. Shortly after the fire, a newspaper editorial in *Svenska Dagbladet* called on readers to "help build Cyklopen again" (Rayman and Gudmundson 2008). The editorialists wrote:

> We put a five-hundred-crown note [approximately €50] in Cyklopen's bank account. We urge everyone who wants to see a free cultural life to do the same. That does not mean we agree with every word spoken within the walls, or that we believe that those who are active there will like ours. But the years of

work put into Cyklopen should not have been in vain. (Rayman and Gudmundson 2008)

The authors are clear: they may not agree with autonomous politics. But with this editorial, the act of supporting Cyklopen became a way of showing support for "a free cultural life," a value that the editorialists assume is shared by Swedish readers of all political backgrounds. Members of Kulturkampanjen appeared at meetings and events around Stockholm to solicit ideas and volunteers for beginning work on Cyklopen 2.0. As I observed these meetings, I expected activists to issue imperatives intended to bring about action ("We must . . ." or "We need to . . ."). Instead, they invited people to speak about a contingent future open to multiple possibilities, asking, "What do you hope to see?" Projective verbs such as "wish," "want," and "hope" appear frequently in activist narratives. For example, one volunteer writes:

> I *want* more groups of curious and committed people to get to create something that is what they dream about. And I *want* there to be more space in which racism, homophobia, and anti-feminism are condemned as severely as they should be. I *wish* for more room where you may be and think radically. . . . That's everything that I see in the Cyklopen and all that I *hope* it will be. ("Berättelser om Cyklopen" 2012, emphasis added)

Rather than being predictive (e.g., "We will" or "We can . . ."), the verbs in this narrative point toward a future that is open-ended and fluid. The last sentence in particular is an excellent example of how prefiguration is rooted in the present ("That's everything that I see in Cyklopen . . .") *and* projected into the future (". . . and all that I hope it will be") simultaneously.

The arson could not have been predicted, nor could the international outpouring of support—especially from unlikely sources. As these events unfolded, they shaped a sense of what was possible for people involved with Cyklopen. Activists built a social center with no money, little knowledge about building, and multiple zoning and planning hurdles. The arson that destroyed it was decried nationally and internationally as a crime against freedom of culture and expression and generated massive financial and political support. For a group that began by getting kicked out of squat after squat, this would have seemed impossible from the start. With the aid of funding from all over Europe, building Cyklopen 2.0 began in the summer of 2011 on a new patch of land in Högdalen, not far from the old location (see Radio Sweden 2012). The building itself is polished and wildly colorful, sided in transparent plastic sheets of green, yellow, purple, and fuchsia (see Figure 3.9). Its futuristic appearance is a startling sight in the natural setting in which it stands. The abundance of resources is apparent in the new design, a stark contrast to the assemblage of found materials of the previous building. The transparency of the walls symbolizes the principles of a place as a "free cultural center" where "anyone who subscribes to the values of direct democracy and gender equality has a standing invitation" (Borg 2013). Practically speaking, it also makes it possible for anyone inside to see out, important given that the first building was destroyed.

Activists with Kulturkampanjen displayed a *volitional* orientation to the future. When people spoke about the future, they spoke about themselves as agents of change. Their orientation was no doubt shaped by massive public support, previous success, and their perception of the future as contingent. Susana said, "I volunteer with Cyklopen *in order to* create a free zone in an increasingly commercialized and gentrified city" (emphasis added). Similarly, Lars said, "I want to do this [build] *in order to* imagine what an alternative city life can look like" (emphasis added). This is what Alfred Schütz (1951) refers to as "the in-order-to motive" (future-oriented speech) rather than "the because-motive" (speech oriented to the past) (163). People spoke about rebuilding Cyklopen "in order to" create a new place, not "because" the other place had burned down.

Volitional orientation also shows up as language "that offer[s] characterizations of the future and ways in which we move towards it" (Mische 2014, 454). Volunteers at Cyklopen write and speak about the building process as a collective journey forward. Johanna says that the promise of Cyklopen 2.0 is "the opportunity to acquire new skills and bring to life abilities that have been dormant. And the meeting with other individuals of different ages and different experiences but with a common goal." In this comment, Johanna points to

Figure 3.9 Top: Cyklopen 1.0 (2007–2008) Bottom: Cyklopen 2.0 (2013–Present) (Credit: Cyklopen)

social movement actors as actively acquiring skills and abilities that will enable a collective journey toward a common goal. Similarly, Susana writes that a building is important because it houses "everything possible we want to create out of our ideas." In this comment, Susana speaks to both contingency (possibility) and volition (collectively creating something new).

Other volunteers at Cyklopen 2.0 talked about how the building process showed them that social movements can effect urban change. This perception is crucial for social movement action because how participants conceive of the future (as a struggle, a risk, a goal, or a crisis, for example) shapes action. One volunteer writes, "[Cyklopen 2.0] gives me hope that the city is not just a frame around our lives but affects [us] and can be affected. It is constantly open to change" ("Berättelser om Cyklopen," 2012). Susana's comment about how she learned how people can "create a free zone in an increasingly commercialized and gentrified city" similarly recognizes not only a future open to change but social movements as active agents of change. Hopes of a future open to possibilities and a sense of efficacy are the building blocks of social change. Cyklopen represents the materialization of dreams and imaginaries about what how the city—and the world—could look in the future. The professional look and clean lines of Cyklopen 2.0 lend the building a sense of solidity and permanence in the landscape. Because the building represents a "place where ideas and dreams about a different kind of society are taken seriously," the strength and permanence of those "ideas and dreams" also become embedded in the landscape.

Conclusion

Social centers are prefigurative places oriented toward the future but also places where people draw upon the *past* to theorize about that future. While activists admire the kind of movement culture that old labor movement created in the late nineteenth and early twentieth centuries, these places are now operated by the state. The state, they say, highlights folk culture in these places and, in operating them as conference centers, prioritizes capitalist enterprise over their beginnings as social movement places. They identify their creation of social centers as derived from the same ideals that these early movements held as important: self-management and freedom from state control. In creating social centers such as Utkanten, Cyklopen, and Underjorden, activists reject engaging in politics via formal institutions, conforming to social norms, and bureaucratic forms of organization that they link to "Swedishness." These places become the cultural hubs of radical leftist movements because they lend a sense of continuity to movement histories, cultural norms, and values.

Welfare retrenchment of the past has created anxiety about uncertain futures, inspiring activists to "stir things up collectively" in the hopes of creating better futures for themselves, both individually and collectively. Scene places are important in these efforts because they are where activists experiment with cultural ideas, norms, and practices that fall outside the boundaries of what they see as a rigid and conformist culture that foreclose possibilities for change. Ideas, norms, and practices are then circulated within the scene and inscribed on the built environment. In these ways, the norms and practices of the movement become embedded in place, lending them a sense of durability that activists hope will carry on into the future.

None of these social centers exist in the same forms as they did when they were established, which exemplifies the shifting and ephemeral nature of scenes. Eviction, arson, and conflicts with authorities (e.g., police, local governments) have forced these places to move and find new ways to survive. This, some scholar-activists argue, "diverts a huge investment of activist time, energy and resources away from the real fight for public space" and leads to projects "built upon compromise, constrained by legal hurdles and enshrined in unnecessary bureaucracy" (Hodkinson and Chatterton 2006, 313). However, it also shows the enduring importance of place for autonomous movements. While none of these social centers are the same today, they still exist, whether in new buildings, in temporary locations, or in the form of new scene places spawned by the ideas, norms, and practices created in them. Despite the "hurdles" they face, activists persist in seeking out new places.

Additionally, the troubles activists encountered while creating and managing social centers gave rise to renewed efforts to claim the right to the city, which I will detail in the next chapter. Instead of focusing their attention on accessing a single building, activists redirected their energy to appropriating urban space more generally by organizing street festivals, squatting buildings, and demanding their right to participate in the (re)development of urban neighborhoods. In this way, the ideas, norms, and practices that are produced in social centers are diffused to other scene places, such as cafés and bookshops, and—in the case of Malmö—to the neighborhood more broadly. These highlight the importance of place—with special attention to geographical location—for establishing social movement continuity, linking the past, present, and future.

4

City Solidarity

The Right to the City in Malmö

A city loses its soul when this continuity is broken. It
begins with little changes you suddenly notice in your
own neighborhood. . . . These changes are not only visible,
they reshape our everyday routines. (Zukin 2010)

On a sunny spring day in 2010, I first visited the Möllevången
neighborhood in central Malmö. At the heart of the neighborhood is Folkets Park (the People's Park), a primary gathering spot and green space. As visitors walk through the park's main
entrance, they are greeted by a description of the park's history. Originally called Möllevångsparken, the park was renamed Folkets Park
in 1891 when the Social Democratic labor movement bought the park
from a local merchant. Folkets Park then became the starting and
ending point for labor movement demonstrations and an important
place for recreation, where "openness, freedom of speech, and cooperation were stressed" by movement leaders (Ståhl 2005, 19; also
Pries, Jönsson, and Mitchell 2020). Markers of the labor movement
dot the landscape of the park, from busts of leading social democratic
figures to a large fountain shaped like a rose, the symbol of the Social Democratic Party. Once the city of Malmö bought the park from
the Social Democrats in 1976, authorities sought to depoliticize the

This chapter is derived in part from an article published in *Social Movement Studies*,
2020, copyright Taylor & Francis, available online: https://www.tandfonline.com/doi/
10.1080/14742837.2020.1798752.

park. The local newspaper, *Sydsvenskan*, reports that park managers between the 1980s and early 2000s claimed that "the Social Democratic stamp remains in people's minds and it is not good. We must be clear that that is history, the park's future is something else" (Orrenius 2003). A new campaign to revamp the park began in 2004 and brought in vendors such as the Stockholm-based music club Debaser and a Ben and Jerry's ice cream stand. Rules governing the park increased: no cycling in the park, no walking on the grass (in some areas), and no handing out flyers. For autonomous activists, the changes in the park are emblematic of changes in the neighborhood of Möllevången more broadly: increased social control, commercialization, and depoliticization of a neighborhood with strong social movement roots.

Paradoxically, the gentrification of Möllevången provided structural conditions conducive to the emergence of a strong social movement scene. A strong social movement scene, according to the spatial dimensions that I outline in Chapter 1, is *central* (relative to the central business district), *concentrated* (in one neighborhood or part of a city), and *visible* (represented by signs and symbols). Because Möllevången was an "undesirable" neighborhood in the early to mid-2000s, autonomous activists were able to find affordable spaces in a centrally located neighborhood fairly easily. By the time of my fieldwork, this had begun to change, with activist groups being priced out by increased rents or evicted by landlords eager to appeal to affluent newcomers.

In addition to available space, the early phase of gentrification is a time when people and groups compete to define to whom the neighborhood belongs and how the neighborhood should look in the future. This is evident in the remarks of park managers who claimed that the social democratic origins of Folkets Park were part of the past and "the park's future is something else." Using creative, place-based activism, autonomous movements demanded a voice in shaping the future of Möllevången. Autonomous movements appropriated urban space (squatting, spray-painting the sidewalks, holding street festivals) and called for local participation in decision making about changes to the neighborhood (the "commercialization" of the local park). In this chapter, I highlight three projects that show

how the ideas and practices of the autonomous scene spilled out into the streets, parks, and squares of the neighborhood of Möllevången. These projects included the Möllevång Festival, an annual street festival; Stad Solidar (City Solidarity), a land occupation on an empty block in Möllevången; and Kontrapunkt, a political and artistic social center that represents a more permanent autonomous intervention in the landscape of the neighborhood. For activists in Malmö, much more was at stake than losing access to buildings. They worry about losing "their" neighborhood entirely.

I begin this chapter with an account of the gentrification process in Möllevången, from 1994 to the end of my fieldwork in 2011, with emphases on the infrastructural, demographic, and cultural changes in the neighborhood. Then, using three place-based projects—a street festival, land occupation, and a social center—I illustrate how the gentrification process was conducive to the development of a strong scene in Malmö. I do not wish to suggest an overly structural account of the scene, so I also emphasize the creativity, optimism, and future-oriented spirit of autonomous movements in Malmö.

The Beginning of Gentrification in Möllevången

The Möllevång Group (Möllevångsgruppen or MG) is a neighborhood association formed by neighborhood residents in 1994. The group's website describes the neighborhood at that time as "a well-known area with major social problems such as littering, irresponsible landlords, an environment that was not child-friendly, and widespread criminality" (Möllevångsgruppen 2010a). For several years the efforts of the group focused on improving the neighborhood's cleanliness and safety. The original goals of the group were to create "comfort and community in the neighborhood," while activities focused on "housing questions, children and youth, integration and cultural and environmental questions" (Möllevångsgruppen 2010a). For example, the group undertook a campaign to "create more pleasant courtyards" in the neighborhood. During this campaign, "a bunch of enthusiastic architects and landscape architecture students surveyed the neighborhood courtyards in [Möllevången], made suggestions for improvement together with the tenants, and managed, in some cases, to persuade property owners to implement the plans" (Möllevångsgruppen 2010a). In 1996, national newspaper *Svenska Dagbladet* reported that "regular Malmö residents are moving out of Möllevången. . . . Those who have moved in are mostly addicts" (Malmö City Library). The area's reputation then became that it was "dangerous, criminal, and full of drugs" (Malmö City Library), and in 2001 surveillance cameras were installed by the city around the main square to discourage crime. In the ten years that followed, infrastructural changes in Malmö, including a new bridge and tunnel system, coupled with efforts of an active neighborhood association and a thriving cultural scene, began to change the look and feel of Möllevången.

The opening of Malmö University in 1998 gave young people a reason to move to Malmö and gave the city and local entrepreneurs a new population to which to appeal. On its website, Malmö University takes credit for "playing a [sic] important role in the transformation of Malmö from an industrial town to a center of learning" (Malmö University 2013).

Two years later, the city of Malmö began making efforts to revamp its image following the opening of the Öresund[1] bridge in the year 2000. The bridge stretches 2.5 miles over the sound between Malmö and Copenhagen. In the years since the bridge opened, Malmö has gone from being a rusty industrial center to a hub of cultural activity. The city's connection to Copenhagen initiated a marketing campaign to establish the Öresund region as a creative hub in northern Europe. Just before the bridge opened in the year 2000, "the Danish and Swedish governments proudly presented a common plan for the future of the cross-border area under the promising title *Øresund— A Region is Born*" (Hospers 2006, 1024). Employing a creative class strategy (Florida 2002, 2013, 2017), a committee consisting of politicians and bureaucrats from each country began a branding campaign to attract business investors, tourists, and creative professionals to the region (Hospers 2006). One economic study claims that "next to London and Paris, the Øresund [region] has gained recognition as

---

1. I have used the Swedish spelling "Öresund" to maintain consistency with Swedish spelling throughout the book. The Danish and Norwegian "Øresund" is more common in English language scholarship on the region.

one of the top three 'hot spots' in Europe in the youthful branch of the knowledge economy" (Hospers and Pen 2008, 267). However, for its residents "[the region] is artificially created by a group of politicians and does not reflect the feeling the majority of the inhabitants have . . . that it is an 'imagined space,'" not something to which they feel a sense of belonging (Hospers 2006, 1028).

According to local residents, infrastructural and cultural changes in Möllevången—"Möllan" colloquially—have contributed to their anxieties about increasing rents, lack of housing, segregation, and destruction of the character of the neighborhood. A 2002 short film titled "Möllevången—Farewell?" (*Möllevången—Adjö?*) chronicles neighborhood residents' views on how the neighborhood was beginning to change (RåFilm 2002). In the film, we meet Kerstin, a member of the Möllevång Group (MG), the local neighborhood association, as she stands in Möllevångstorget, the main plaza and marketplace in the area. With a concerned look on her face, she looks out over the neighborhood's main plaza and says, "Möllevången is a very unique neighborhood. It's a nice area to live in and it's special. But the city is changing." Agnes, a resident of Möllan for eight years, articulates more specific concerns:

> I'm afraid that [Möllan] will become high rents and segregated and "oh let's go down to the corner and have a cappuccino." That would make me puke, make me go crazy because Möllevången is such a special place in Sweden and a special neighborhood.

Agnes emphasizes that Möllan is a "special" place in both the city and in Sweden because unlike class-based and ethnic segregation found in other large cities, people of different ethnic backgrounds and social classes inhabit the neighborhood. In her view, the changes in the neighborhood portend high rents, segregation, and posh coffee bars, which she believes would destroy the character of Möllan.

These changes must be understood in the context of "creative city" policies enacted by city authorities to attract professional workers in the larger Öresund region, including Copenhagen, the cosmopolitan Danish capital. A business report from the city planning office describes much the same process: "The city of Malmö is engaged in a series of economic development initiatives regarding development, creative environments, and meeting places for entrepreneurship" (Malmö Stadskontoret 2012, 26). Hans, an activist involved in several local activist projects, says,

> Malmö has slowly—well, not slowly actually—pretty quickly gone from an industrial city to being marketed [by the city] as a very creative one where a lot of young people move to work. And it's been like that for the last five years or something. Ten years, really, but even more in the past five.

Helena, another local activist, concurs: "Over the past five to ten years, people have moved from all over Sweden to Malmö. And most of them want to live around this area [Möllevången] 'cause this where the cultural life is most active." Changes in the commercial landscape, combined with the neighborhood improvement initiatives, marked the area as desirable for people moving into the city as well as for "commercial investment that will upgrade services and raise rents" (Zukin et al. 2009, 48).

From the perspective of autonomous activists, creative city policies are gentrification with a cool, artsy façade. In response, activist groups began to mobilize in 2006. By 2012, autonomous movements had created a rich oppositional culture in Möllevången in response to the gentrification of Möllevången. As I walked along the eastern edge of Folkets Park—the heart of Möllevången—I encountered anticapitalist stickers on drainpipes and flyers for a squatting project on the wall bordering the park. A local café featured a bulletin board filled with colorful flyers issuing a call to "Stop the Commercialization of Folkets Park" by "city politicians and private investors with dollar signs in their eyes." It was tacked next to a flyer for the Möllevång Festival, a street festival "for the people, by the people."

The visibility of these signs and symbols serves several purposes. First, they are crucial for advertising events. Second, it allows one to physically experience the scene by walking on the spray-painted sidewalk, passing by flyers, and traveling under banners. Third, these signs and symbols are "a construction of a sense of locality and territoriality, as a means of demarcation and appropriation of public space" (Gerbaudo 2014, 248). In a gentrifying neighborhood, claims over territory (both physically and discursively) are an important part of the process (Brown-Saracino 2009).

In December 2010, the link between Sweden and Denmark stretched even farther into Malmö when the City Tunnel opened. The City Tunnel is a rail line linking Copenhagen and Malmö and includes a new station called Triangeln (the Triangle), located just a few blocks from the main square in Möllevången (see Höök 2012). According to a 2012 report about economic development in the city, the Öresund bridge "has played an important role in the growth of the Öresund region" and "the City Tunnel is projected to have a similar role in [developing] a competitive wider region" (Malmö Stadskontoret 2012). The hope that the City Tunnel will bring a brighter future to Malmö is evident in the architecture of the station itself, which is a dome made of angular glass that sparkles when the sun glints off its geometric form.

Most of the activists that I interviewed expressed concern about how the new station at the Triangle will impact the neighborhood. Tanja says, "I think the biggest change now is the station here [Triangeln]. It's a big change because then the neighborhood becomes attractive to a whole other kind of people and the cost of living here will probably go up." When pressed about who the "other people" are, she said, "People who think that huge shopping malls and more parking spaces are good things." Hans, another local activist, said, "Soon this area will be all students and people with money." Similarly, Ulrika says, "The City Tunnel will change who lives and works in the neighborhood. Soon, a lot more professional types will probably live here because the station will make it easy to commute to Copenhagen for work. They also plan on building a bunch of offices around [the Triangle], so that will make it attractive to professionals, too, because they can walk to work."

City planners project that the City Tunnel will bolster the effects of the Öresund Bridge in developing an economically competitive region (Malmö Stadskontoret 2012). Current and future projects aimed at further economic development in the city include the Emporia shopping center (three floors, containing two hundred shops, cafés, and restaurants); a new structure housing a convention center, concert hall, and hotel; development of the university hospital; and plans for a metro line between Copenhagen and Malmö and the rebuilding of three existing shopping centers, including one at the Triangle (Malmö Stadskontoret 2012). These projects were proudly advertised on placards at the station, representing two competing visions for the future of the neighborhood: an economically sound future to city planners and an ominous symbol of commercialization to activists.

Neighborhood improvement projects also had major effects—many of which were unintended. Everyone I interviewed in Malmö cited visible, aesthetic changes as evidence of social changes in the neighborhood. Visible changes in the commercial landscape of a city block or area "[enhance] the quality of life of the new urban middle class" while making others uncomfortable (Zukin et al. 2009, 48). For example, as one activist, Theo, says, "The grimy bars don't exist anymore. Now it's all cocktail bars [. . .] all the bars around here feel so . . . posh. More people with money live here now. It wasn't always so 'nice' to live in Möllevången." Theo's comments are about the visible changes in the landscape but also about feeling like an outsider in one's own neighborhood where "people with money" live. Visible changes in the landscape create a sense of displacement not as "a spatial fact"—many people I interviewed still lived and worked in the neighborhood—but as "a loss of a sense of place" (Davidson and Lees 2010, 403). Population statistics support these anecdotal claims. While the number of residents in the neighborhood has not increased dramatically over the past ten years, the average income of residents has increased (Malmö Stad 2000, 2008, 2014).

The Möllevång Group's efforts to clean up their neighborhood, combined with the influx of new populations looking for affordable housing, began to change Möllan's image from a dangerous neighborhood to a desirable one. The city of Malmö recognized Möllan as a symbol of community spirit and cultural vitality and began promoting it as a cultural district. Current members of the Möllevång Group acknowledge that the group's earlier activities have had unintended effects. By employing a community-based approach to making the neighborhood cleaner, safer, and more lively, they also made it a desirable place to be—and impossible for some residents to afford. Fredrik, who was born in the neighborhood and is a current member of the MG, says, "In the beginning, [the Möllevång Group] started in order to get rid of the feeling of not being safe, they wanted to make the neighborhood a little nicer. But I don't think they saw the consequences that would come with those changes. People started leaving, people who *were* [Möllevången] in some way."

Place-Based Politics of the Autonomous Scene

At the time of my fieldwork, the autonomous scene in Malmö consisted of dozens of activist groups that operated in places such as an activist café, a radical feminist bookstore, an art space, and a social center housed in a former warehouse, as well as temporary autonomous places like street festivals, land squatting projects, and protest sites. These places were all located just blocks from one another and clustered around Folkets Park in the heart of Möllevången (Figure 4.1).

In response to the infrastructural and cultural changes in Möllevången, autonomous movements began to mobilize in 2006. They used the places, practices, and activities of the scene to claim territory *and* to leverage a discursive opportunity to shape the direction of a changing neighborhood. Autonomous activists appropriated space in former factories and warehouses, rented storefronts, and empty city blocks. They showed up at new construction sites in protest and eventually took over the local neighborhood association. At the same time, they also created multiple opportunities for other local residents (who were not activists) to participate in decision-making processes about how the neighborhood would develop in the future. In addition to benefitting from favorable structural conditions, autonomous activists in Malmö were also creative and tactically savvy. They did not rely solely on tried-and-true protest tactics like demonstrations, instead opting to create community art projects and interactive installations to generate greater community participation in their activities.

The Möllevång Festival (Möllevångsfestivalen)

In 2006, autonomous activists began to plan the first annual Möllevång Festival, a street festival in the heart of the neighborhood, that

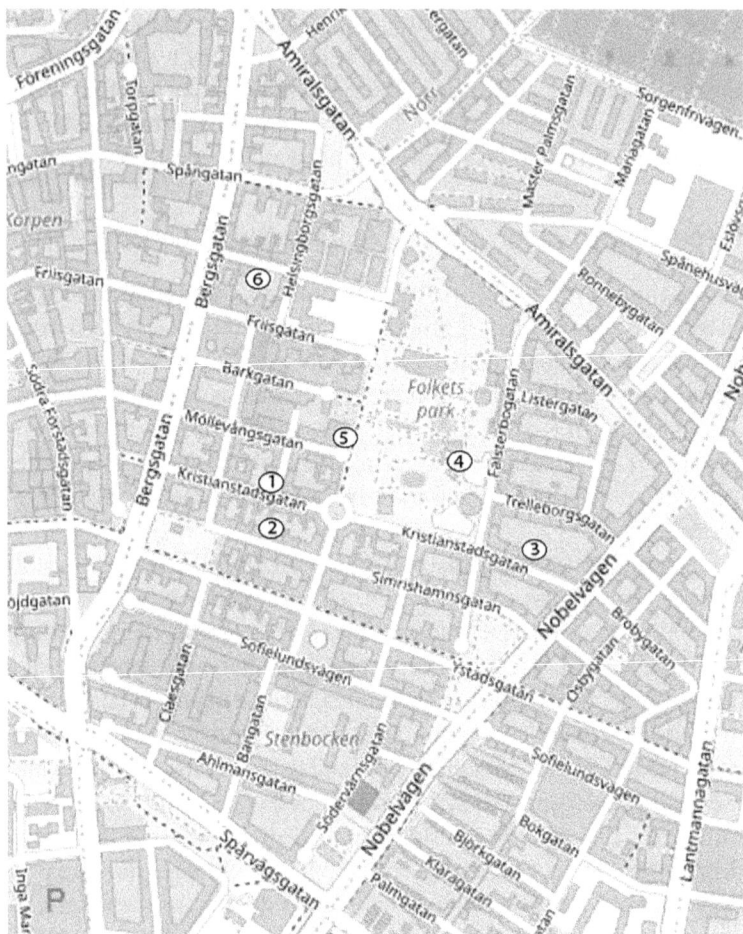

Figure 4.1 The autonomous scene in Möllevången during fieldwork period. In chronological order: 1. Glassfabriken; 2. the Möllevång Festival; 3. Amalthea Feminist Bookshop and Café; 4. the place in Folkets Park that activists tried unsuccessfully to access; 5. the Möllevång Group offices; 6. the site of Stad Solidar. (Credit: OpenStreetMap contributors, licensed under Open Database License, www.openstreetmap.org)

took place every summer until 2010. The festival is a clear example of how activists staked territorial and discursive claims on territory in a changing neighborhood. The festival operated without a formal permit from city authorities for five years. According to organizers, when the festival began to rival Malmöfestivalen, the annual festival hosted by the city, they were told that they had to apply for the requisite permits, which the group could not afford. In its final year (2010), the festival took on a decidedly more political atmosphere, and gentrification was a central target of its political goals (see Olsson 2010a). The goals of the Möllevång Festival were to get neighborhood residents involved in local cultural events and to assert a "right to the city" through both *participation* and *appropriation* of space. This is clearly articulated in the description of the festival:

> Möllevången residents play the central role in the work of the Möllevång Festival and they give weight to the festival if they engage in and develop the events into a festival of streets, courtyards, and squares. This commitment is the seed of a greater local democracy in the area where people take a greater part in the design of both the physical and social environment. (Möllevångsfestivalen 2010)

By calling on the inhabitants of the neighborhood to expand the festival beyond its official boundaries by taking over "streets, courtyards, and squares," organizers of the festival advocate appropriation of public space in response to commercial gentrification of the area. The call for local residents to "take a greater part in the design of both the physical and social environment" is a clear example of how activists created a forum for other local residents to participate in defining the neighborhood on their own terms. The festival encouraged participants to shape the built environment. Taken together, activists argued, appropriation of space and participation in defining the neighborhood create "the seeds of a greater local democracy."

The festival's main areas were called the Marketplace, the Green Street (denoting environmentalism), and the Red Street (denoting leftist politics) (Figure 4.2). The Marketplace streets had the feeling of many North American art festivals where local artists and vendors sell their wares—jewelry, textiles, street food—and engage in small

Figure 4.2 Map of the Möllevång Festival (Möllevångsfestivalen) 2010. With this map, activists conceptualize neighborhood space according to political ("red") and environmental ("green") concerns. In doing so, they produce a new, alternative vision of the neighborhood.

talk with passersby. The Green Street consisted of "music, workshops, and conversation about an ecologically sustainable city and world" (Möllevångsfestivalen 2010). The street was lined with tables staffed by people from organizations such as Greenpeace and the Society for Nature Conservation (Naturskyddsföreningen). There was a "snack stop" offering fresh produce at a table encouraging people to "go vegetarian" and a blender powered by a bicycle on which festivalgoers could make a smoothie simply by pedaling. The Red Street "focused on political and social questions through information, film, music, and conversation." Large banners hung over the Red Street urging locals to "work together against the gentrification of Möllevången." The street—like all of the streets—was lined with tables shaded by tents under which activists sat on couches and chatted with one another and passersby.

One tactic employed by activists to stake a claim on territory during the festival was the use of living room furniture—sofas, chairs, coffee tables—in the streets (see Figure 4.3). It began as something festival organizers did, but the practice caught on with local residents who eventually pulled their own couches and chairs out into

Figure 4.3 Living room in the streets, Möllevång Festival 2010

the streets. The festival organizers initially put the furniture on the streets as a strategic move intended to "reclaim the streets" in a creative way that reflects the character of the neighborhood. Alex explains:

> During the whole festival we tried to make [the streets] like a living room—'cause it is our living room. Most people living in Möllevången, that's where we meet people, just through open windows, talking, meeting in the streets. . . . And so we filled the streets with sofas and chairs and carpets and tried to make it nice. . . . *This* is the right to the city, just to show that this is a part of my home. It's not just a place where cars should drive and I should walk on the sidewalk, but we're taking some control of the city in a way.

Fredrik envisions the neighborhood streets as an extension of residents' homes, a social space where people meet and greet one another on a daily basis. Similarly, Erika said, "We really wanted to focus on [creating] atmosphere and feeling. We wanted people to see the festival as a big living room where people can meet and spend time together." The organizers of the festival are residents of Möllan and, through this action, they hoped to bring others from the neighborhood together in the streets. Placing their furniture in the streets was obviously an appropriation of physical space, but it also embodied a vision of the future in which social interactions between neighbors take center stage. Hanna explains that, while festival organizers staged furniture in the streets initially, it inspired other residents to follow suit: "People [attending the festival] thought it was the people living on those streets who had taken their furniture out of their apartments, which it wasn't, but once we put out furniture, they took out theirs, too, to support what we were doing." This action and reaction, say Alex and Hanna, are examples of how the festival organizers hoped to get their neighbors to "take a larger part in the design of both the physical and social environments" (Möllevångsfestivalen 2010).

While the city-as-living-room tactic represents a unique approach to appropriating space, which is more often accomplished by tactics such as squatting or demonstrations, the idea of the city as living room is "common in Swedish planning discourse" (C. Thörn 2011, 998; see also Castell, Danielsson and Stehn 2008). Swedish sociologist Catharina Thörn (2011, 998) uses the example of a city campaign called "THINK—Take Care of Our Common Living Room" to discuss how public-space-as-living-room is represented in the city's campaign:

> The CBD [central business district] is depicted as a private living room. On one of the images a middle-aged, well-dressed couple greets a guest into their elegant home captioned with "Welcome to Our Home." The woman holds a tray and glasses of champagne in her hands, yet the floor of the living room is littered with cans, paper, old food, etc. The adjacent text reads that "it is time to think about what the streets look like when tourists come to town" and ends with the catchphrase "Take care of our common living room."

Both activist and urban planning notions of city-as-living-room draw on language about a shared home, though their goals in drawing on this familiar idea are different. The Möllevång Festival organizers use public space as an extension of inhabitants' homes in order to make them feel empowered by shaping the landscape—even if temporarily. Advertising campaigns like the one quoted earlier tell inhabitants to "think about what the streets look like when tourists come to town," taking focus *away* from city inhabitants. Instead, such campaigns reinforce "perceptions of public space as commodities and the importance of creating consumer-friendly environments" (C. Thörn 2011, 998).

The city-as-living-room tactic employed by the organizers of the Möllevång Festival drew the attention of city authorities. The city of Malmö also hosts a festival, Malmöfestivalen, each summer. According to Alex and Ebba, organizers for the city's festival wanted to rent furniture from the Möllevång Festival. Alex interpreted it as a strategic move to shut down the Möllevång Festival:

> We've made a festival that people actually liked, in some cases better than Malmöfestivalen 'cause with the city, everything is by the books, everything is order and everything is in rows. There's no atmosphere that feels like you're just living. It's very structured. So Malmöfestivalen wanted to take the atmosphere we created. . . . And when it didn't work for them, they started saying things like we had it much easier because we didn't have to operate by the same rules that they do, and then they put the same requirements on us as they did on Malmöfestivalen. And they have a *huge* budget. We have like 5 percent of their budget, if that. So, we can't afford to keep it going.

According to Alex, the Möllevång Festival embodied a community spirit and sense of togetherness that was absent from the larger city festival, which he characterizes as overly structured—a common autonomous critique of public life in Swedish cities. Alex saw the request to rent furniture as attempted co-optation of the Möllevång Festival. He interprets the requirements of city permitting as a means of squashing the festival by making it financially impossible for the Möllevång Festival to carry on. Ebba told me a similar story:

> We tried to tell them [city authorities], we all work voluntarily and this [festival] gathers together all the groups that

make Malmö what you promote as "a cultural city." We are not working professionally, so we have to do this on our terms. And you can't *use* us to attract people and then make our lives miserable.

The battle over festivals, it seems, is representative of competing narratives over the future Möllevången. The city of Malmö wants to promote economic development in order to draw new knowledge workers and industry to the city. Autonomous activists see these moves as calculated efforts to increase social control, commercialization, and depoliticization of "their" neighborhood. As a neighborhood in transition, Möllevången is up for grabs and competing groups make claims on space—both territorial and discursive.

City Solidarity (Stad Solidar)

Malmö activists were tactically savvy, employing several projects and actions aimed squarely at competing notions of the future brought about by gentrification. In addition to the Möllevång Festival, the project Stad Solidar is a good example of tactical innovation in the Malmö scene. In October 2010, activists built a small city of huts (Figure 4.4), which they dubbed Stad Solidar (City Solidarity). Stad Solidar was "a political art project that is equal parts an interactive art installation and an act of civil disobedience and protest against gentrification of Möllevången, specifically against the planned building of [market-based] cooperative housing on the empty lot by Möllevång School" (Stad Solidar 2010; see also Olsson 2010b). The lot was owned by Peab, one of the largest construction and civil engineering companies in the Nordic region. Their plan for the block was to build cooperative housing[2] on the site. Stad Solidar argued that building properties for purchase rather than renting means that only people

---

2. Housing in Möllevången consists primarily of small apartments. Sixty-two percent of apartments in Möllan are either classic "worker apartments" (one room and a kitchen), while 39 percent are one-bedroom apartments (Malmö Stad 2008). As of January 2012, 75 percent of these apartments remained rental properties, but since 2004, rental properties are increasingly being converted into cooperatives (Höök 2012).

Figure 4.4 Stad Solidar, Malmö, November 2010 (Credit: Stad Solidar)

who can afford to buy apartments will be welcomed to the neighborhood. These changes in housing tenure, they argue, threaten current
residents of the neighborhood, who could not afford to buy apartments, and therefore the future of the neighborhood.

Stad Solidar created opportunities for direct action in opposition
to the gentrification process. The Stad Solidar blog invited readers to
"admire constructive and beautiful activism, have a chat with those
of us who are there, or build your own version of a dream society"
(Stad Solidar 2010). By creating such a project, Stad Solidar not only
critiqued the lack of available avenues for participation in city planning, they also created possibilities for people to participate in shaping how the city could look in the future. The group's blog reads,
"Sometimes one gets tired of nagging, rhetoric, and buzzwords like
'democracy.' . . . It can be really great to take a hammer and hit a nail
in the name of what one believes in" (Stad Solidar, 2010). Through appropriating space and creating a future-oriented mini-city, local residents used creativity—and hammers—as tools to fight gentrification.

As part of the process of defining potential futures of the neighborhood, Stad Solidar also created a vision of a new way of life for

some participants. In a particularly lyrical description of this kind of vision, one activist wrote about her evening at the site as a kind of urban imaginary:

> Fires burned in several places. I could hear laughter, music, and the sound of hammers. Dear friends and acquaintances hung out in the shadows and I got a hug here and a kiss there. Warmth spread both in my heart and my stomach. Imagine if it could always be possible to be met by this when one comes home after a full day at work.

This description of her evening at Stad Solidar is not about the physical appropriation of space but about being part of creating a place in which she was surrounded by sounds of creative endeavors (music, building), happiness (laughter), and friends who greeted one another. This example mirrors activists' descriptions of the neighborhood, in some ways (e.g., as a place where people greet each other on the street and through the windows of their homes) and elicited in this participant an emotional response to an urban imaginary in which this kind of experience was part of daily life.

The centrality, concentration, and visibility of the project—as part of a broader scene—helped bolster both the scene and the movement. Interview data and Stad Solidar's daily dispatches reveal the number and variety of people engaged in the project. Jesper, an activist with Stad Solidar, told me, "Kids from the school would come out on their lunch breaks and make their own cardboard houses. They were so excited!" Stad Solidar's blog tells readers about Hilda, a seven-year-old student at the school next door, who came by the lot every day. After five days, she brought her mother and a friend and they built a golden cardboard house, inhabited by stuffed Santa Clauses and bumblebees. On Stad Solidar's Facebook page, Bodil, a forty-five-year-old Möllevången resident, writes,

> I am a 45-year-old Swedish woman who has never lived in any other way than on the poverty line. I am one of those who will be forced to move somewhere else if Möllevången and vicinity become "nicer." I am one of those who drag down the status of the area. . . . Even though you [Stad Solidar] see the cold

hard truth and the major injustices and inequalities that are growing [in the neighborhood], you have used a constructive, creative, and inspiring strategy for making visible what is happening. THANK YOU!

In her heartfelt message to the group, Bodil foresees her future in the neighborhood as limited because people living on the poverty line "drag down the status of the area" in its transformation to being an entertainment area for upwardly mobile middle-class families. What's more, she applauds the group's use of creativity as a means of raising important questions about the future of the neighborhood and its current residents, thanking them for putting a spotlight on these issues. Markus, another "builder" at Stad Solidar, told me, "Even senior citizens walking past would stop and comment that this was a very good initiative—which is a very tough group to appeal to—but they understood it straight away. We didn't have to have much discussion about gentrification and so on, they just got it." Commenting on the variety of people involved in the project, Lina says, "If we had called it an occupation, the classic kind with hardcore activists in black clothes and punk music and language, the reaction would have been totally different. We never would have managed to get big support in the community." These examples show that the project met its goal of gathering a large base of support in the community that was diverse in age, occupation, social class, and gender.

Despite cold temperatures and roofs that caved under snow, Stad Solidar lasted through the winter, until March 2011 when it was torn down by Peab's bulldozers. A newspaper report (Anjou 2011) paints a dreary picture of the destruction:

> Different kinds of waste lay in piles in different places, crushed glass was everywhere. Shattered furniture was piled next to clothing that had been left behind, soaked by rainwater. Some dumpsters stood in a parking place waiting to be filled. A handful of huts were still standing and looked to be inhabited.

One member of Stad Solidar says that at least one of the huts was inhabited by a homeless man until just before Christmas. Markus expresses surprise at the quick destruction: "It's too bad that Peab tore them down without warning about it or those who live in the huts. I haven't heard if Peab even has a building permit [yet]. They could have taken it a little easy." In response, Per Wickström, the project development leader at Peab, said, "We are required to keep the site in good condition. The artwork and some buildings have already been taken away by the group. Only some of the outlying huts are left" (Anjou 2011). Building a new cooperative apartment building began on the site of Stad Solidar in the summer of 2011.

Momentum for the Future

Physical places are important to autonomous groups because they give a sense of vitality to social movement norms, practices, and histories. Through projects such as the Möllevång Festival and Stad Solidar, activists felt that they had accomplished the goals of raising public debates about gentrification and enabling local residents to actively participate in shaping public space and debates about the future of the neighborhood. What was lacking was a sense of continuity or momentum after the festival or land occupation ended. To remedy this, Malmö activists established Kontrapunkt, a "cultural and social center" that houses a dozen social movement and cultural groups. Autonomous activists also became a more active part of the Möllevång Group, the neighborhood association that has been the "voice" of Möllevången since 1994. Through establishing places where politics and culture could come together on a regular basis, activists felt as though the work they accomplished with the festival and Stad Solidar would become embedded in the social and geographical landscape of Möllevången for several years to come.

Kontrapunkt (2009-2019)

The collaboration between self-identified political and cultural groups during the Festival and Stad Solidar created a desire among activists to create a place where this collaboration could continue throughout the year. Jesper points out that the festival was great, but "even though a lot of good things come out of it, we felt like it wasn't filling all the needs we thought we needed in the movement, in Malmö." One of the "needs" that was not being met by any other groups, in his view, was "to bring the cultural people and the political people together."[3] The collaboration that worked so well for the Right to the City projects is one that activists hoped to foster more continuously. So, according to Kerstin, "the idea came up to have a place where we'd bring the cultural groups and the political groups, where we could raise money for different projects . . . yeah, where we could satisfy the needs of different groups and to share resources." The impetus to create a new place was not only to keep the spirit of the festival going all year but to foster continued collaboration between the "political" and "cultural" groups in the city. The locale, located in a warehouse district just south of Möllan, was called Kontrapunkt.

The word "Kontrapunkt" (Counterpoint) is a musical term referring to voices that are woven together to create a composition. In a similar fashion, the cultural and social center of the same name brings together different cultural and political groups to create a collective entity. The name also has an oppositional edge when activists use the prefix "counter" to denote resistance. For example, when I arrived at Kontrapunkt in 2011, building materials lay in piles in every room and the sounds of hammering echoed in the halls. When I entered, a few people greeted me, and I was offered a cup of coffee and seated on a couch—one that had sat on the streets during the last Möllevång Festival. As I looked around, I noticed flyers, printed in bright yellow and red, that featured a fist around a hammer and the words "Kontra Bygg" (Counter Build). This is a clear message of opposition to gentrification and increased commercial building by "counter building" a place to foster opposition to these social forces.

At Kontrapunkt I met Ulrika, a filmmaker working with a film collective that meets at Kontrapunkt. Other "house groups"—that is, groups that had an affiliation and/or meeting space at Kontrapunkt—include the Research Department (the hacker group formerly housed at Utkanten); Klädoteket, a "clothing library" that operates a free shop; Isolera Israel, the Palestinian solidarity network that spray-paints their web address on the sidewalks in Möllan. These are just

<hr>

3. See also Jämte, Lundstedt, and Wennerhag (2020) for a similar distinction between "lifestylists" and "workerists" (27–28).

a few of the dozen groups that are associated with the place, but they represent the diverse interests of Kontrapunkt, both political and cultural. Markus explained that anarchist social centers of the past have been temporary and perhaps a bit exclusionary:

> There have been different, similar places in Malmö, but most of them have been very anarchist, punk type places and most of them have lasted maximum, maybe one [or] two years. Some have been just a few months and it's been the anarchist movement that's done it.

Kontrapunkt is similar to places like Utkanten in that it is a social center that aims to bring together a diverse range of social movements. However, Markus points out that they lack continuity, much the same as the Möllevång Festival. His comment about social centers being "anarchist, punk type places" implies that perhaps these places might not appeal to people who do not identify with anarchist politics. After all, one of the goals of Kontrapunkt is to bring "synergy" to a variety of people and groups. Similarly, Kerstin says,

> When we started Möllevångsfestivalen, which are a lot of the same people that are involved in Kontrapunkt, the idea was to, like, reach a broader target audience than just political groups . . . to make it a little bit more accessible for people who may not be politically aware or have that interest.

It's not only activists to whom the people at Kontrapunkt hope to appeal but also to a "broader audience" of people who may not identify as activists—or politically interested at all. Although Kontrapunkt is part of the autonomous scene in the city, they hope to keep diffusing the ideas and practices of the festival to a wider audience beyond activists.

By calling themselves a "cultural and social center," activists and artists at Kontrapunkt continue the theme of Möllevång Festival and Stad Solidar by trying to bring together culture and politics. Jesper says that—once again—this created some skepticism among some political activists about wanting to get involved with Kontrapunkt:

In Sweden, people are very locked in a kind of . . . square way of thinking. Even if you're politically active, people have trouble seeing alternative ways of thinking. The means you have demonstrations or manifestations or some kind of action. [. . .] People are just repeating the actions of previous movements. There's no step forward. So [our] hope, and the idea of Kontrapunkt, is to step up the ambition and get people to organize in a more creative way.

Like many people involved in autonomous milieus, Jesper points to how social movements in Sweden sometimes operate within a very limited idea of what constitutes political action. Namely, social movements engage in demonstrations that look and feel very much like the demonstrations they had previously. Markus says, "We don't want to go out there and say, 'this is what Kontrapunkt is going to be.' . . . We want to leave it open. We're working on it slowly and we want to get people to realize the values of this place for their own lives." As organizers and builders, the people I met at Kontrapunkt were very wary about attaching any one identity to the place in order to keep it open to people and possibilities for action.

On the other hand, they do fulfill some of the same roles and encourage the same kinds of activities of the social centers I describe in Chapter 3. For example, in a pamphlet titled "Kontra Bygg" (Counter Build), the building plans include a kitchen, office spaces for photocopying, a bike workshop, a library, meeting rooms, stages with sound systems, an exercise room where dance and theater troupes can practice, and much more. The very title of the pamphlet— "Counter Build"—hints at using countercultural or "alternative" values to build something new. On their website, they list their goals in the following way:

To strengthen and develop grassroots social movements
To create strong, active, and creative social engagement using
    culture as a tool
To be a cultural platform that furthers free and unestablished
    cultural life
To transmit knowledge, competency, and resources to and between local cultural and collective activities

> Through meetings, collaboration and exchange promote multi-culturalism, integration, and community between people from different backgrounds and social groups (Kontrapunkt Collective 2012)

These goals bear some resemblance to those of the social center Utkanten that I discussed in Chapter 3. For example, Kontrapunkt's interest in developing collaboration, cultural independence, and collectivity are like Utkanten's emphasis on independence, self-determination, and "creating culture without boundaries." Unlike Utkanten, however, their goals speak to the process of diffusion, by aiming to "transmit knowledge, competency, and resources to and between local cultural and collective activities" from Kontrapunkt to the wider community. Additionally, they define that wider community as "people from different backgrounds and social groups," something that reflects the composition of the neighborhood and its transition from old to new.

Between 2015 and 2019 Kontrapunkt frequently made news headlines for their activities, particularly when they began operating a refugee welcome center out of their space. They provided soup kitchens, bunk beds, medical help, and transportation to Göteborg and Stockholm for newly arrived migrants. This created an ongoing dispute with their landlord and the city planning office because Kontrapunkt did not have the requisite permits for these activities (see Larsson 2017). In January 2019, the dispute came to a head and Kontrapunkt was forced to leave the premises. In April of the same year, the group started a new campaign to rebuild in a new location. Permits, construction delays, and legal and financial woes ultimately stymied the project by February 2020 (Kontrapunkt Collective 2020). In an article in the anarchist magazine *Brand*, the collective writes, "We moved into our premises with a vision to gather all the activities we previously did under one roof. . . . The opportunity to meet and organize is fundamental to democracy and organizations in Malmö are hard hit by both the lack of, and the closure of, existing meeting places. . . . We give up the premises but we never give up the fight! We have seen what is possible when we use our collective forces together" (Kontrapunkt Collective 2020).

The Möllevång Group (Möllevångsgruppen)

Another avenue that activists pursued in order to establish a more continuous presence in the neighborhood was via the neighborhood association, the Möllevång Group. Though the group formed in 1994 to address littering and beautification, its goals changed as the neighborhood changed. The core organizers of the Möllevång Festival were part of the group already, but the year after the festival ended, autonomous activists became a more vocal and active majority in the group. By becoming a vocal and active majority in a long-lasting, established neighborhood group, activists secured a durable position in the neighborhood, both in the form of a physical place (the MG office is located on the edge of the park—see Figure 4.1) and by becoming "the voice" of the neighborhood in its dealings with the city of Malmö.

In 2011, the goals of the group took on a decidedly political tone. The group is described on the website only as "a new group of enthusiasts," and their statement begins, "We want the Möllevång Group to become a vibrant social center in Möllan, open to everyone but for left-wing movements and local associations especially." In this opening line, they explicitly locate MG within in the autonomous left scene by expressing the desire for the group's meeting place—located on the edge of Folkets Park—to be a social center. They further specify that they are *especially* welcoming of left-wing activists and local association members.

The social movement character of the revamped group is further underscored when they describe their approach as "a grassroots perspective, i.e. we see things from below, from the residents' point of view. We pursue the questions that the residents feel are important." In order to use the MG meeting place to show a film or have a meeting or discussion group, all one has to do is show up to one of the group's public meetings, which are held every Monday evening. These meetings, they write, are open to everyone—including anyone who is "just curious" about the group (Möllevångsgruppen 2010b). In this way, the practices and policies of the MG offices have essentially become a new social center.

Jesper, who has worked with the group on a few projects in the past, says, "I want there to be more public engagement [in Möllan].

That's what the group hopefully will do now, go out in the streets, invite people in, get people engaged. [What happens in the neighborhood] should be based on what they want." Although the group's site and Jesper's comments say that anyone and everyone are welcome, they suggest that there are boundaries when they draw specific attention to left-wing movements and local associations.

In the group's written materials, as well as my interviews with group members and neighborhood residents, changes in the composition, goals, and tone of the group are a response to the social and cultural changes happening in the neighborhood. In a statement titled "What do we do?" the group writes,

> Möllan has changed a lot since Möllevång Group's start, from being a neighborhood afflicted with problems into a thriving neighborhood with a vibrant cultural scene and active community engagement. Möllan today is arguably Malmö's most popular district as a result of this transformation. But as the district has become more and more attractive rents have risen, rental housing has disappeared and the shops that characterized Möllan have found it hard to stay here. The dreaded gentrification has the neighborhood in its grip. That Möllan will change is inevitable, but what Möllevång group now fights for is change based on the ideas and desires of Möllevången's residents themselves. Get involved today, tomorrow may be too late!

The group recognizes that the neighborhood's transformation follows a similar, "inevitable" trajectory of many gentrifying cities: local efforts to clean up a neighborhood make it more attractive to students and young artists. The demand for bars, cafés, restaurants, music venues, and galleries makes it attractive to real estate developers and new residents, which creates higher rents, fewer available rental properties, and new kinds of cultural spaces. By calling on inhabitants of the neighborhood to act, they issue a call to demand the right to the city. They do not call for gentrification to stop. Rather, they ask local inhabitants to be part of shaping the changes that will inevitably happen in the neighborhood.

The revamping of the Möllevång Group allowed activists to take the goals, methods, and efforts of the two-day Möllevång Festival and institutionalize them in the form of a physical place that has had a continuous presence in Möllan since the mid-1990s. The "new" MG group is representative of how the Right to the City projects help spur the development of new social movement scene places. Activists take the ideas of the scene, diffuse them into the neighborhood, and then use the momentum from those projects to establish new scene locations. In this way, autonomous values, as expressed by the right to the city, are further embedded in the neighborhood landscape.

Conclusion

Changes in the commercial landscape, infrastructure, housing options, and aesthetics have been ongoing since the late 1990s in Möllevången. Autonomous activists are among the loudest voices protesting these changes, arguing that the neighborhood is unique in its history and the strong relationships among residents. Beginning in 2006, autonomous groups began to mobilize against gentrification of the neighborhood using creative tactics aimed at staking territorial claims and increasing participation of residents in decision making about Möllegvången's future.

The Möllevång Festival and Stad Solidar are examples of how gentrifying neighborhoods are conducive to strong movement scenes through access to available space. The Möllevång Festival would not have been possible if city authorities had required activists to obtain expensive permits from city authorities—indeed, this was the reason the festival eventually ended. Stad Solidar would not have happened if not for the development project planned for an empty lot in a central part of the neighborhood. These projects allowed local residents to participate in actions and discussions about the future of the neighborhood, a process made urgent by the ongoing gentrification of the area.

The scene in Malmö was centrally located in the city and concentrated in the gentrifying neighborhood of Möllevången, in part due to available space and affordable rent. With places located on main streets and the political symbolism that marked the landscape, the scene was highly visible to passersby and laid claim to territory in a neighborhood in flux. The scene was also concentrated with scene places being tightly clustered together in one area of the city. Activists felt invested in the neighborhood and stressed the importance of being part of an engaged community. Activists organized several direct actions to enable neighborhood residents to have a voice in shaping the environment of Möllevången to reflect their wants and needs. Taken together, a strong scene was made possible by favorable structural conditions, given Möllevången's status as a neighborhood in flux, tactical creativity on the part of activists, and support from locals.

5

Where Is the Movement?

The Spatiality of Social Movement Scenes

O n a dark evening in the winter of 2009, I attended a meeting of activists at Café Hängmattan, a Brazilian-themed cafe in Södermalm. This meeting was not advertised but convened via word of mouth. The small room that had been reserved for the meeting was packed with people, and I was surprised, given the lack of action I had seen during my first few months in the city. Activists gathered to discuss possible squatting actions, city space, and the importance of self-managed social movement places. The mix of people was diverse in age, interests, and experience. Some people spoke nostalgically about Reclaim the Streets actions in the 1990s. A member of Kulturkampanjen said they were soliciting volunteers and suggestions for what people wanted to see as they moved forward on rebuilding Cyklopen 2.0, the next generation of the social center in Högdalen. Another person talked about the squatting action at Aspuddsbadet, a bathhouse in the southern suburbs. Finally, a member of the autonomous action group Alarm Stockholm gave an impassioned speech about the importance of focusing on urban issues such

Portions of Chapter 5 appeared in Creasap, K. (2016). "Finding the movement: the geographies of social movement scenes," *International Journal of Sociology and Social Policy*, vol. 36, no. 11/12, pp. 792–807.

as commercialization of city centers and diminishing public space in the city. This meeting was emblematic of the Stockholm autonomous scene. People took turns speaking about their groups and activities, but there were no plans by the end of the meeting. While all of these projects are vaguely connected in that they all deal with how city space is used and by whom, there were no concrete directions for action that resulted from the meeting.

The scenes in Stockholm and Göteborg looked very different than the one in Malmö presented in the last chapter. While Malmö had a *strong scene*, in Stockholm, there was a *fragile scene* consisting of a loosely knit network of activists and a network of places that was geographically dispersed, in the suburbs, and primarily formed around temporary spaces and single events. In Göteborg, there was a *fledgling scene* consisting of a tight-knit network of autonomous activists that formed around a social center, temporary spaces and actions that were difficult to find and socially "closed."

Scenes vary spatially—according to centrality, concentration, and visibility—which has different outcomes for local movements. In the last chapter, I presented the autonomous scene in Malmö as an example of a *strong* scene in which scene places are close to the central business district, concentrated within a few blocks, and highly visible in claiming territory. In this chapter, I present *fragile* and *fledgling* scenes as two more kinds of scenes. These dimensions and scene typologies are by no means exhaustive. But they do add specificity to the concept of a social movement scene while remaining dynamic enough to apply to a wide variety of scene configurations and locales.

Differing configurations of social movement scenes are partially shaped by the structural conditions of the cities in which they form. As the last chapter shows, Malmö activists felt emotionally connected to a neighborhood because of its labor movement history, carefree character, rich cultural life, and sociocultural heterogeneity. Threats posed by gentrification of the area energized autonomous movements. Their efforts were aimed at solidifying their place in a unique neighborhood that they loved. In Stockholm and Göteborg, the analogous neighborhoods, Södermalm and Haga, respectively, gentrified decades ago. Social movements no longer have a place in the landscapes of these cities.

Comparisons of the strong scene in Malmö and the fledgling and fragile scenes in Göteborg and Stockholm highlight that certain features and qualities of place lend both social movement scenes resilience over time. As the case of Malmö/Möllevången showed, concentration, centrality, and visibility all worked together to create a strong autonomous scene. Place making is "an iterative, evolutionary process of defining not just boundaries or territories, but the rules and norms against which socio-spatial practices are understood" (Pierce, Martin, and Murphy 2010, 58). Therefore, having a range of places or "contact points" is important, but the proximity and centrality of those points makes social interactions in these places "frequent and routine" (Nicholls 2009, 85). Making activism part of everyday life in a neighborhood helped activists in Malmö diffuse the ideas, norms, and practices to a wide variety of people. Consistent face-to-face interactions also allow diverse activist networks to become more cooperative, communicative, and open to new ideas, as the example of the "political vs. cultural people" in the last chapter illustrates.

The scenes in Stockholm and Göteborg differ in density of activist networks and spatial dimensions. In Stockholm, activist networks are loose and disconnected. In Göteborg, activist networks are dense to the point of being inaccessible to outsiders. These scenes also differ spatially, along the dimensions of concentration, centrality, and visibility. Spread out over a large area in the southern suburbs, the scene in Stockholm is geographically diffuse, peripheral, not visible, and *geographically* difficult to find since it coalesces around temporary spaces and events. In Göteborg, the scene has relative proximity but is peripheral, not visible, and geographically difficult to access.

These fragile and fledgling scene configurations have different outcomes for social movements and urban neighborhoods than strong scenes do. In Malmö, actions were geared toward securing a future in the central city, in the hopes of giving the movement—and scene—resilience that would secure their place in the neighborhood and move them toward a newly imagined future. In Stockholm, the fragile scene reinforced the loose networks and fleeting relationships between activists, thereby limiting their potential to move forward collectively because of a lack of collective energy and affective bonds. In Göteborg, the fledgling scene produced exclusivity, limiting their movement by making it difficult for new actors to access.

Most activists in Stockholm and Göteborg were not focused on momentum for the future but on the challenges of the present. Therefore, they engaged in actions that served immediate needs: getting people together in one place (Stockholm) or trying to get new people to join their movement (Göteborg). They did so primarily through squatting actions and single events (e.g., the Anarchist Book Fair), actions that had temporary effects. The lack of routine, consistent interactions that are fostered by a scene with a variety of places that have concentration, centrality, and visibility limited their momentum and possibilities for the future.

In the next section, I present the history of two neighborhoods (Södermalm/Stockholm and Haga/Göteborg) with similar histories as Möllevången in Malmö. All three were working-class enclaves and home to labor movements in the late nineteenth and early twentieth centuries, making them attractive to autonomous social movements that admire labor movement culture. The urban processes that have shaped neighborhood change are also very similar to those in Malmö/Möllevången, but the transformations in Södermalm/Stockholm and Haga/Göteborg happened decades ago. Therefore, while there has been a continuous social movement presence in Malmö, social movements in Stockholm and Göteborg struggle to find their places in the city—both literally and figuratively. This will set the stage for the next section, in which I describe the social movement scenes in each city, highlighting the dimensions of proximity and centrality.

Then I turn to the autonomous spaces and places in each city. I begin with a description of Kafé 44, an anarchist café, info shop, and concert venue that has been operating in Stockholm since 1976. This place is important as a reference point for autonomous movements in both Stockholm and Göteborg. A radical institution, Kafé 44 is critiqued by activists for its "established" character; they seek to create something different. In the final sections of the chapter, I turn to the outcomes of the scenes in both Stockholm and Göteborg. In Stockholm, activists described a lack of collective energy and affective bonds as a result of a lack of geographic concentration in which to develop such dynamics. In Göteborg, activists worried about the exclusivity and "closed" nature of the fledgling not-quite-a-scene as a result of the tight-knit groups.

Urban Change in Stockholm and Göteborg

At a community meeting in November 2009, members of the urban action group Alarm Stockholm passed out a pamphlet titled "Stockholm Is Ruined," which points to Södermalm, the neighborhood in which the meeting took place, as an example of what they see as negative urban change:

> Södermalm has undergone an extreme change from having been a working-class neighborhood with a strong left-wing and alternative character to quickly adapting to the needs of an affluent middle class. (Alarm Stockholm 2007a)

The story Alarm Stockholm writes about Södermalm/Stockholm is strikingly similar to the story that Möllevången/Malmö activists tell about their neighborhood. In this passage, the group points to Södermalm as a working-class, leftist enclave that is now a middle-class, apolitical neighborhood catering to the newly arrived "creative class." High rents as well as expensive bars and boutiques make the borough undesirable (and uninhabitable) for leftist groups similar to those that inhabited the neighborhood in previous decades.

Haga, a central neighborhood in Göteborg, shares a similar history. Once the home of labor movements, Haga—like Södermalm/Stockholm—was marked for demolition as a "slum area" in the 1960s. Artists and young students moved into the district, lending the area a countercultural ambiance (H. Thörn 2012b). In the early 1970s, neighborhood movements[1] (*byalagsrörelser*) began to organize in response to building demolitions in both Stockholm and Göteborg. Young urban activists and older, working-class residents of the neighborhood launched a campaign in the 1970s to save Haga from destruction on the grounds that it was a "historically valuable old working class neighborhood" (H. Thörn 2012b, 161). Haga activists—like those in Malmö—contributed to the reversal of the neighborhood's place identity from a slum to a creative and trendy area.

In both Stockholm and Göteborg, historic neighborhoods associated with working-class pasts became important places worth

---

1. For a history of these movements, see Chapter 2.

"saving" for leftist movements from the 1970s to the 1990s. While partially interested in conserving the physical landscape of these neighborhoods, activists also tried, in varying degrees, to establish some sort of leftist culture. These histories laid the groundwork for contemporary autonomous communities in each city today. In Stockholm, where a radical political scene never really established itself in Södermalm during this time, activist groups lack connections and communication. In Göteborg, where an autonomous movement scene declined after the transformation of Haga, activist networks operate in temporary, often underground places on the outskirts of town.

Stockholm: Södermalm and the Southern Suburbs

Like Möllevången/Malmö, Södermalm ("Söder") was an industrial zone and working-class borough from the late nineteenth century to the 1970s. When families began to leave the inner city for newly developed suburbs in the 1960s, students and artists—many of them politically leftist or anti-establishment—began to move into Söder because of the availability of cheap housing. In the early 1970s, rent regulations were changed by the city, giving landlords power to negotiate rents and incentive to rebuild or modernize their properties. As a result, many apartment buildings in Söder were slated for demolition. These conditions made the neighborhood attractive to new social movements, as "there were many cheap dwellings, attracting particularly students. For many of them, politically leftist or just anti-establishment, Söder's popular and radical tradition was an extra asset" (Franzén 2005, 63).

The New Left—particularly environmental activists—engaged in occasional street actions and squatting, but more importantly, they joined forces with the borough's tenants' association (Hyresgäst-föreningens Södermalmsavdelning or HFS). Throughout the 1970s, the infusion of autonomous politics into HFS led to support for autonomous political projects, such as communal squats and an annual street festival called the Söder Festival (akin to the Möllevång Festival in Malmö, only thirty years earlier) (Franzén 2005).

The primary focus of HFS was preserving old apartment buildings and defending the rights of tenants, *not* appropriating space and creating autonomous places. In the long run, these movements did

Figure 5.1 Map of Stockholm scene: 1. Kafé 44; 2. Cyklopen; 3. squat in Liljeholmen; 4. squat in Aspudden; 5. the Anarchist Book Fair. (Credit: OpenStreetMap contributors, licensed under Open Database License, www.openstreet map.org)

not establish themselves as part of Södermalm's place identity. Sociologist Mats Franzén (2005) suggests three reasons why this is the case. First, there was a lack of available space. Södermalm/Stockholm deindustrialized slowly, with factories closing one by one. The city was efficient in turning those places into housing or administrative buildings at a steady pace, leaving no available space for alternative movement cultures. In other cities, where many factories closed at once, there was an abundance of available space that was largely viewed by property owners as useless—and therefore ripe for squatting.[2] Second, the message of the movement was one of preservation, not change. Specifically, due to the focus on tenants' rights, their message was about keeping the buildings, people, and neighborhoods as they were, not opening up possibilities for new initiatives. Third, as I have shown in previous chapters, the Swedish system of government is relatively closed to outside actors. Since many of the buildings in Södermalm were owned by the municipal government, they decided what to do with them—without input from local groups.

Stockholm activists—particularly those from Alarm Stockholm—talk about the past nostalgically. Anders from Alarm Stockholm says, "We [people in Alarm] used to hang out in Söder a lot. There was a thick layer of dirt on the windowsills on Götgatan [a major street in the neighborhood] and there were lots of secondhand music stores and stuff. Today Götgatan is full of expensive shops." In their manifesto, Alarm Stockholm (2007b) writes, "It's unavoidable that a city has a center and we in Alarm have not given up on the inner city—the center of a city belongs to everyone." The group draws on the past in an attempt to provoke action in the central city, particularly Södermalm, which they see as a neighborhood for social movements, given its history as a labor and squatting movement zone.

Today, Södermalm is arguably Stockholm's trendiest borough. According to the Stockholm city website, the area is characterized by "a rich cultural life," "trendy and unusual boutiques," pubs, restaurants, and "strong social engagement among residents" (Visit Sweden 2013). The district has gained international recognition since the suc-

2. After World War II, many European countries recognized squatters' rights, given the level of destruction to available housing during the war. Since Sweden was neutral, this was not the case there.

cess of Stieg Larsson's best-selling Millennium series of novels, which have been adapted into films in both Swedish and English. The main characters of the series reside in Söder, making it a popular tourist destination—so popular, in fact, that the Stockholm tourist bureau offers maps for a Stieg Larsson Millennium Tour, a walking guide based on the novels (Visit Sweden 2013).

In a transcript of a conversation titled "The Struggle Has Just Begun," leftist activist America Vera-Savala comments that "Söder in Stockholm is romanticized and seen as an alternative to the bourgeois inner city. [But] there are no special people who live there, there's no special culture any longer. We must stop romanticizing and create politics from our current situation" (Hedlund and Gagge 2009, 9). These comments suggest that left-wing activists talk nostalgically about Södermalm as the home of alternative cultures, when, in fact, "there's no special culture [there] any longer." Alarm Stockholm writes that they "have not given up on the inner city," but *Direkt Aktion* suggests that maybe they should. Rather than longing for how the neighborhood *used to be* and focusing on the past, these comments suggest that activists "create politics" in the present.

Many activists I met in Stockholm talked about the suburbs to the south of the city as the next frontier (Figure 5.1). In 2009, activists issued a call for a community meeting at a coffee shop in Södermalm to discuss possible Right to the City actions. For many people in attendance, the link between the city and the suburbs was becoming an important question because now that the inner city was gentrified, development would start outside the city center. Just as activist networks of the past responded to urban development projects in Söder/Stockholm, contemporary activists are responding to them in the suburbs using the same tactics: squatting and discussion groups. During my fieldwork, there were squatting actions in Liljeholmen and Aspudden, suburbs just south of Södermalm. Cyklopen, the city's social center, is located in Högdalen, farther south of the city center. Recently, the action group Allt åt Alla held a week of discussion groups titled "Sideways City: City Struggle in the Southern Suburbs." The goal was "a transfer of knowledge between the southern suburbs," an effort to bring together disparate groups over the planned building of new highways that would connect them geographically (Allt åt Alla 2014).

What these efforts lack are *centrality, visibility,* and/or *proximity.* Squatting actions happen outside the centers of cities or even suburban communities, often in industrial areas that do not get a lot of foot traffic from residents or neighbors. Squats are often raided by police shortly after they become publicized, making them difficult to access if one is not an activist insider. All of these projects take place in the southern suburbs but are spread apart so that there is no connection between them—geographically or in terms of activist networks that enact them.

While Alarm Stockholm fights to hold on to the central city—and social movement histories—other activist networks look to the southern suburbs as the site for the next wave of protest. In part, this move is influenced by the past. The processes against which social movements protested in previous decades are now taking shape in suburban areas, not the inner city. Therefore, activists see the future of those areas as inevitable, but they seek to intervene in those processes. Some groups do so using similar tactics (squatting), while others suggest seeking out new forms of action to "create politics from our current situation." These comments recognize a future that is "not simply a possibility, but is something which is already present in the configuration of the game" (Adkins 2009, 88). These calls for action recognize practical action based on the present as the best road forward.

Göteborg: From Haga to Gamlestaden

Like Södermalm/Stockholm and Möllevången/Malmö, Haga was an important place to leftist social movements in Göteborg's past. The neighborhood is located just across a canal that defines the city center; its history as a working-class enclave began in the 1840s when new industry emerged in Göteborg. In the 1920s, the neighborhood became "a stronghold for the workers' movement" (H. Thörn 2012a, 199), a legacy that is evident today only in the close proximity of the local People's House. In the 1930s, local social democratic groups called for the demolition of Haga, which "represented a part of working-class history that was shameful—a 'slum' associated with poverty and disease" (H. Thörn 2012a, 204). In the Social Democrats' sweeping urban renewal efforts of the postwar period, Haga

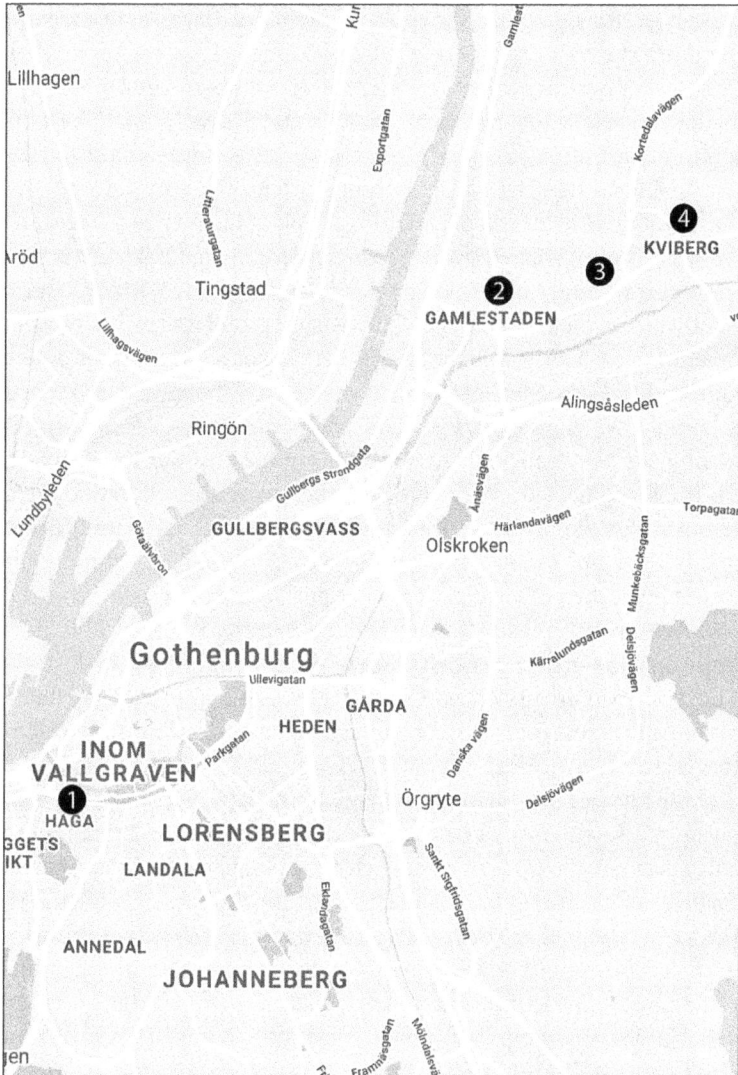

Figure 5.2 Map of Göteborg scene: 1. Haga; 2. Gamlestaden (Underjorden); 3. the sites of Kampen om Göteborg; 4. squat at Kviberg. (Credit: OpenStreetMap contributors, licensed under Open Database License, www.openstreetmap.org.)

was slated for demolition by the municipality. Because of plans to demolish the area, Haga was "a rundown inner-city area impaired by long-term physical neglect" by the 1960s (Holmberg 2002, 63). In the early 1970s, a movement emerged to "save Haga." These efforts were led on two fronts: by the municipal museum and the Haga Group (Hagagruppen), a neighborhood group. These groups are partially responsible for establishing Haga's place identity as a "workers' district." Building conservationist Ingrid Holmberg (2002) notes that the municipal museum's guidebook describes Haga as a "worker's area," but then goes on to explain how the neighborhood was rather socially mixed, historically. While the images in the book show factory workers and seamstresses, the text says that the neighborhood was also home to middle-class innkeepers, grocers, and homeowners. A museum official says the overall goal of renovations in the area was to "maintain the impression of a worker's area from the turn of the century, so there remains a possibility to imagine aspects of the hard and poor life that was lived there" (quoted in Holmberg 2002, 69). These examples illustrate that the museum played an important role in establishing the place identity of Haga as a working-class enclave of historical importance in Göteborg—a city that takes pride in its working-class history.

From the early 1970s to the late 1980s, social movements also played an important role in reversing Haga's reputation from a slum to a place of historical value (H. Thörn 2012b). Artists, students, and hippies began moving into Haga in the late 1960s, attracted by cheap rents, which began to change the neighborhood's reputation. Influenced by the work of Henri Lefebvre, neighborhood movements formed, consisting—as in Södermalm/Stockholm—of students in the social sciences, architecture, and urban planning. By linking up with "official political discourse of historic preservation" (as exemplified by the museum), activists helped to (re)define Haga's identity as a historic working-class enclave worthy of cultural preservation (H. Thörn 2012b, 161).

In the late 1980s, a new generation of squatters moved into the neighborhood. This generation—resembling the punk rock, anarchist aesthetic of today's squatting movements—switched the emphasis away from conservation and toward creating communal living spaces. Despite differing political goals (conservation of buildings vs. alternative living), the newcomers were welcomed by the older generation of activists because they breathed new life into a dying leftist culture in the neighborhood. These groups wanted to preserve both the physical landscape of the neighborhood and a countercultural way of life in Haga.

In 1988, a group of squatters moved into a building across the street from Haga Church. They called themselves *husnallarna*, a term chosen for its double meaning as "teddy bears in the house" (symbolizing their commitment to nonviolence) as well as "those who snatch houses" (squatters) (H. Thörn 2012a). The goal of the *husnallarna* was to create communal forms of living. A journalist from the national newspaper *Dagens Nyheter* visited the house, which she described in the following way: "The stairways smell like cat urine and the building is, simply put, a real dump. [However,] the apartment is a little gem. [Squatters] have furnished it with finds from dumpsters and flea markets. It is simple, but beautiful and tidy" (Berglund 1988, 32). The description contrasts Haga's image as a slum with "the new Haga" that presses on outside the building. As one squatter puts it, "'the new Haga' [is] beautiful, attractive, expensive, and for a *whole different kind of people*" (Berglund 1988, 32, emphasis added). The "different kind of people" are middle-class gentrifiers, attracted to the historic charm of Haga's working class past.[3] By the early 1990s, both the historic preservationists and countercultural activists were history, too.

Today Haga retains its historical charm with the mix of old brick and even older wooden buildings, as well as cobblestone streets and sidewalks. It is an expensive residential area and home to several small boutiques and cafés along the main drag, while smaller side streets are oddly quiet, even in the busy summer months when tourists flock to the area. Nearby Järntorget (iron square) remains a busy meeting place and transportation hub, surrounded by symbols of the area's labor history (Folkets Hus, union-related educational organizations, and the Social Democrats' bookstore) as well as global capitalism (Burger King).

Like their counterparts in Stockholm, contemporary autonomous networks in Göteborg have begun to turn their attention to areas outside the city center (Figure 5.2). The social center Underjorden

---

3. The phrase "attractive and for a whole different kind of people" is a verbatim description of Möllevången in the early 2000s, given in Chapter 4 by Ulrika, an activist in Malmö.

was located in the industrial area Gamlestaden, northeast of the city center. As I described in Chapter 3, Gamlestaden is an industrial area organized around a factory (SKF) that makes ball bearings. Tomas described it as "not really the suburbs, but it's not the center of the city either. It's in between, it's very mixed." Tomas describes the neighborhood as "mixed," referring to its mix of residential and industrial, city and suburb, and mixed housing tenure.

In March 2010, flyers began to appear around Göteborg for a weeklong series of actions called the Battle over Göteborg (Kampen om Göteborg, Figure 5.3). The flyer is a good example of the mixed messages that the Battle over Göteborg produced. This flyer highlights three urban issues: the sale of the flea market to a private individual, autonomous self-management, and changes in housing tenure. The action blog included the following description:

> Gamlestan and Kviberg [a neighboring borough] are undergoing a clear gentrification process. During this week, we will conduct an exhibition and discussion tour in public places throughout northeastern Göteborg, including organizing a concert, holding workshops, conducting a demonstration and more. All with one goal: to show that there is a resistance to the changes people are trying to make in the district and other ideas about how the city should develop.

This description is, in many respects, similar to those written by activists in Malmö that call for the right to the city. The gentrification process is provocation for protests, which took the form of arts, music, and discussions in public places about making urban development processes more participatory. However, these actions also differ in important ways. First, the Battle over Göteborg is a *battle*, creating a boundary of us versus them. Malmö activists made inclusivity a goal for their actions. Second, it is unclear who "we" and "they" are. Göteborg activists by and large do not reside in Gamlestaden or Kviberg. Third, the series of actions were not limited to a clearly defined, central area. The blog highlights Gamlestaden and Kviberg as the sites of the actions, but the actual events happened in different neighborhoods each day. In Malmö, Right to the City actions were limited to a single neighborhood. In Göteborg and Stockholm, suburban

Figure 5.3 Flyer for Battle over Göteborg. It reads "Preserve Kviberg's Market. Battle over Göteborg. March 1–7. Autonomy from Below. Not one more co-op!" (Credit: Source unknown)

protests—like the suburbs themselves—were spread out over a much larger area. Finally, the message of the action was mixed. In Malmö, the messages of Right to the City campaigns were clear: we want a voice in our neighborhood. Battle over Göteborg tried to address too many issues at once—housing, self-managed spaces, and privatization. Although these are all expressions of the right to the city, they did not clearly connect, conceptually or with residents.

Activists in Malmö were able to diffuse the practices of the scene into the neighborhood more broadly using the right to the city because the scene and individuals were part of the neighborhood. In Göteborg and Stockholm, activists have not had a continuous presence in any particular neighborhood. Helena, an activist from the social center Underjorden in Göteborg, says, "We've had some problems at Underjorden. We're not very liked by everyone in the area because we've had parties and we've been noisy and there have been some clashes with the neighbors." The activist presence in Gamlestaden was viewed by neighbors as a nuisance, not an embedded part of the neighborhood. Helena also adds, "It's hard to tell if the area can become like an activist zone because people still live all over town." As she points out—and my data reflect—activists don't live in Gamlestaden, but "all over town." Whereas the scene in Malmö coalesced around a tightly knit community of people and places in close proximity, that is not the case in Göteborg.

Social Movement Scenes

Stockholm: The Fragile Scene

Autonomous scenes in Stockholm consist of affinity groups—loosely knit networks of activists that organize around a single campaign and then disband and gather again for the next project. Most activists in Stockholm attributed the lack of a lively activist scene to the fact that it is the country's largest city, both in population and in land area, making people more spread out and less likely to bump into one another as they do in Malmö, for example. But this factor alone fails to explain why scenes thrive in cities much larger than Stockholm.

When I asked activists in Stockholm to describe the social movement scene in the city, their comments spoke to a lack of connection, visibility, and centrality. Tobias, an anarchist I met by spending time at Kafé 44, says, "Of the political contacts I have, few have really led to friendship or anything like that. We meet at political meetings and events, but it doesn't really go further than that. I don't understand what the reasons are for that, but . . . it's tough." Tobias makes a distinction between the kind of distant, in some cases fleeting, relationships that he has with fellow activists, few of whom become friends. While they engage in activism together, their relationships never develop more.

Mariska, an activist involved in several anarchist initiatives in Stockholm, says that it's not only a lack of interpersonal connections that are missing, but a lack of visibility for activism in the city as well:

> It's actually kind of weird because if you look around, look out there at the internet and the projects going on, there seems to be quite a lot [happening in Stockholm]. Living here? It feels like there isn't. You don't meet those people very much; you aren't confronted with any kind of radical political culture in everyday life in [Stockholm].

Mariska's comment speaks to a lack of visibility and routine interaction among activists that she attributes to a lack of being "confronted" by "radical political culture." This highlights the importance of central places that facilitate routine interaction between people as an important component of scenes.

What Mariska describes was the exactly the quandary I found myself in when I arrived in Stockholm and began searching for people to interview and places to visit. Having done abundant internet research before leaving the United States, I was prepared to find more radical political culture in Stockholm. As Mariska points out, there seemed to be several projects going on in the city—but where were they? Similarly, Mads, one of the organizers of the Anarchist Book Fair in Stockholm, attributes this to a lack of communication among groups:

> A lot people are doing their own projects here and there, but I think if they were better connected and worked together, the overall presence of that scene would be a lot stronger. A lot

of it seems to happen out of the sight of . . . well, pretty much everyone.

Mads acknowledges that there are groups doing activist work in the city, but that they are isolated from one another, contributing to the lack of visibility of the scene and movement. Mariska says that one is not "confronted with radical political culture," and Mads points out that "a lot of [projects] seem to happen out of sight." These comments suggest the importance of social connections and visibility for the production of a social movement scene.

Several people pointed to Cyklopen as having a major impact on the social movement community because it became a central point where people could meet, dream, and feel like part of something greater than themselves. Cyklopen's website includes a page called "Stories about Cyklopen" for which people were asked to share "a memory, a feeling, [or] a reason why places like [Cyklopen] are important" ("Berättelser om Cyklopen" 2012). In response, people wrote passionately about "feeling like part of something bigger than oneself" and "meeting other individuals, with other experiences, but who share a common goal" ("Berättelser om Cyklopen" 2012). These comments point to how "geographic stability enables activists to engage in frequent face-to-face ritual interactions which charge newly established connections with strong emotional power" (Nicholls 2009, 85; see also Collins 2004).

For others, building at Cyklopen was their first foray into social movements. One woman's narrative, for example, recounts how she moved to Högdalen (the suburb where Cyklopen is located) after leaving home. She and her friends "had heard talk about a culture center in the forest where they had super cool parties—parties without a closing time." Going to Cyklopen gave her a feeling of freedom—being away from home, staying out late with her friends, not having her parents tell her what to do. She continues,

A few years later, when I heard that the building had been burned down it came as a shock. Then when I heard about the authorities' lack of action (and sometimes pure malice) regarding getting a new building, I got angry. Really angry. And began to think politically. The fact is that the events surrounding Cyklopen have laid the groundwork for many of my understandings of society and politics. It has helped me understand what a public space is and how important such spaces are.

This narrative describes the importance of Cyklopen as a point of entrance into activism. The feelings of freedom that this writer first experienced at Cyklopen created an emotional attachment to the place itself. The "events surrounding Cyklopen" (the fire, the negotiations to secure a new patch of land) became a way for this writer to learn about local social and political issues alongside others.

Göteborg: The Fledgling Scene

When I arrived in Göteborg in late January 2010, I walked out of the train station, pulling a heavy suitcase through the snow. As I approached Gustav Adolf's Square, I saw the peaks of two white tents rising above protest banners that read "Protest Center AGAINST the Iranian Regime" and "No to Execution" (Figure 5.4). With city hall

Figure 5.4 Protest center in front of Göteborg's city hall

in the background, Gustav Adolf the Great, the seventeenth-century monarch who founded the city in 1621, points to the protest center, commanding passersby to look. Activists handed out flyers and talked to interested onlookers about the executions of two protesters who had been arrested during Iran's national elections in 2009. Within my first five minutes in the city, I saw more visible protest activity than I had in weeks in Stockholm. I was reminded of Mariska's comment that "you aren't confronted with any kind of radical political culture in everyday life in [Stockholm]" and was surprised by the very different message that I was already getting in Göteborg. All around the city center, one sees evidence of radical politics. A flyer titled "DIY Sunday" is plastered on tram stops, inviting the public to "come and hang out!" at a "people's kitchen" and a music show at the local social center Underjorden (see Figure 5.5). The lettering on the flyer is cut-and-pasted and handwritten, creating an aesthetic that is reminiscent of punk rock zines—not that surprising given that the group organizing the day is Spatt, an anarcho-punk collective. A hand-drawn image of a bound and gagged Hitler sends a clear anti-fascist message.

The diversity of protest tactics (squatting, anti-fascist dinners, protest centers) is matched in the diversity of activist identifications. Alex, who is part of the anarcho-punk group Spatt, says, "You have everything from the very hardcore anti-fascists to the really pacifist anti-military people and animal rights and feminists and the queers and everyone's very . . . we have all of these different groups. But they still get along quite well!" Unlike in Stockholm, where people seemed unsure of what other activist groups existed or what they were doing, Alex suggests that not only do people in different groups know each other, but they get along. When I ask Lisa, who is involved in anti-fascist and asylum rights groups, how she sees the differences between Stockholm and Göteborg, she replies,

> I think because in Stockholm it's more . . . it's more . . . people aren't that close in Stockholm or in other cities, like they are in Göteborg. . . . Yeah, I think it's because people are closer to each other. It's a big city, sure, but it's really small for being a big city, so people are really close here and relaxed and trust people more than in Stockholm.

Figure 5.5 DIY Sunday flyer advertising a "people's kitchen" and several bands, hosted by the anarcho-punk collective Spatt (Credit: Spatt)

These comments reinforce the idea that connections between people are what support and nurture a scene, making Göteborg feel "really small for being a big city." Feelings of trust lend Göteborg's community a sense of connection, while in Stockholm, she suggests, people do not share those emotional bonds—a statement that is supported by activists' comments in Stockholm.

Similarly, Sara, a squatter in Göteborg, tells me that there is cooperation among Göteborg's activist networks, despite their different goals or issues:

> We cooperate a lot with other groups too. I know that No One Is Illegal does some things with Revolutionary Front and Antifa too. Even though we have different opinions about stuff, we're more together and doing stuff together, so we trust each other more than people do in Stockholm, for example. . . . People here are closer to each other, I think.

In Stockholm, interviewees pointed to a lack of communication and coordination among activist groups. Sara, however, points out that activist groups deal with issues such as anti-fascism (Antifa), asylum rights (No One Is Illegal), and squatting (Revolutionary Front[4]). She points to events such as music festivals, parties, and protests—all of which are temporary autonomous zones—as places that foster close relationships among activists. Organizing events and spending time together reinforces a sense of trust and camaraderie among people in the community.

Activists in Göteborg pointed out a few places that they saw as important but highlighted that they were temporary and fragmented. Sara said, "It has a lot of potential to, like . . . if people get more connected and work more together, we could have a lot of good stuff." Her answer is representative of several activists I interviewed in Göteborg, who talked about the "potential" for there to be a thriving activist scene in the city, but cohesion and access to places were lacking. Tomas, for example, says,

---

4. Revolutionary Front is a militant organization that also promotes anti-fascism, among other leftist causes, but was actively promoting squatting at this time in Göteborg.

We have this place, Kulturhamnen, which is down by the harbor. I heard that they're closing down now because they can't pay rent, which is sad [because] they've also been trying to make a political place for happenings and such. Then we had Truckstop Alaska. They're not outspoken politically, but they're also a collective arranging gigs who have a big place. They're also an autonomous space, a place where you could arrange gigs, [No One Is] Illegal has had support gigs there. They're also a nice group of people, and it's an alternative place to go to, even if they're not outspokenly political. Otherwise, I dunno.

Tomas, who was active in squatting, Underjorden, and the punk rock music scene in Göteborg, points out a couple of places but notes that Kulturhamnen, an attempt at creating an autonomous place, was forced to close, and Truckstop Alaska was more of a music venue than a social movement place.

Aside from very public protests, it was difficult to find social movements in Göteborg. More centrally located places would help new people and potential activists access the scene. Lena, for example, says,

It feels like there are these small places around, like spread out, but it's hard to find if you don't really know about them. There needs to be something. It would be good to have a central meeting place that's cheap and open for everyone, but still has political information that's a very political place.

Lena highlights that the openness and affordability of places like Truckstop Alaska make such places more accessible but that they should still have a political quality in order to help the social movement community in the city grow. This sentiment is echoed by Rasmus, who told me that he and some friends had been considering starting a queer feminist bookstore in the city center:

Me and some friends are talking about how we need more political spaces, so we've been talking about starting up a café and we want to be quite central in the town because that's a

little bit missing, to have a central place where people might
just pass by and go in randomly, for people who are not politically active or want to be politically active but don't know how.

Rasmus points out the need for "more political space." Like activists
in Stockholm, both Lena and Rasmus point to the importance of visibility and centrality for making the social movement community
more accessible for people as a means of becoming politically active.
While it is not difficult to find signs of protest in the city, access
points to the social movement community are more difficult to find.

Kafe 44: A Radical Institution

When I began my fieldwork in Sweden in 2009, nearly everyone I
met directed me toward Kafé 44, an anarchist café, info shop, and
concert venue in Södermalm. Named for its address (Tjärhovsgatan
44), Kafé 44—just "44" to locals—is a radical institution. Kafé 44 has
been a hub of radical left-wing activity in Söder since 1976, when a
group of artists and architects turned a bottle cap factory into a collective working space. The collective, Kapsylen (the Swedish word for
"bottle cap"), is still alive and well in Söder after nearly thirty-three
years (see Kapsylen 2020).

To get to Kafé 44, I exited the metro at Medborgarplatsen, a major
transportation hub in Söder. Tjärhovsgatan is a narrow, quiet street
that runs parallel to Folkungagatan, the major thoroughfare in area.
Mirroring the fashionable district of SoHo (South of Houston) in New
York, some people refer to this area as SoFo (South of Folkungagatan).
Folkungagatan is lined with high-end furniture boutiques and chain
stores ranging from Indiska (a Nordic clothing store chain) to Pizza
Hut. Based on its trendy appearance, one would never guess that this
area once had a reputation as a place of criminal activity. One block
south, the buildings lining Tjärhovsgatan are old and painted in pas-
tel colors, giving the street a charming, old-fashioned feeling—a re-
minder of what the neighborhood movements of the 1970s succeeded
in preserving. Compared to the bustle of Folkungagatan, this street
was always quiet, with only the noises of distant traffic and leaves
crunching underfoot. Kafé 44 is on the ground floor of the Kapsylen
factory. As I approached for the first time, I saw a black metal door

standing open, revealing a bumper sticker that read "Don't vote . . . it just encourages them" in English. Walking through the front door off the street, I entered INFO, a small radical bookshop in which the walls are lined with shelves of books on anarchism, anti-fascism, feminism, and so on. A single person typically staffs the shop from a small card table in one corner of the room. From there, I went down a small flight of well-worn wooden stairs and entered the seating area of the café. I spent many winter days at the café, working, meeting friends, and conducting interviews. On an average day, music by Leonard Cohen or the Clash will play (sometimes loudly) from the speakers overhead. The tone is generally calm, with a few people hanging out, drinking coffee, or eating lunch.

The café clearly promotes autonomous politics, evident in the symbols that cover every surface in the place, but I never saw the discussion groups, fund-raising parties, or activist meetings that were common in social centers. In addition to the books in the bookshop, one can buy anti-fascist calendars and pamphlets. Virtually every surface of the café (including the bathroom) is covered with flyers, stickers, or graffiti with political messages. An anarchist "A" decorated a chalkboard on one wall. Next to the honey, sugar, and milk, I found flyers for upcoming demonstrations, zines about environmental issues, and postcards advertising alternative commercial venues in the city. A black poster on the wall by the kitchen reads "Stateless. No leaders, no nations, no borders."

The place has been a popular hangout for leftists since the late 1970s. It retains a sense of enchantment among young activists and punk rock fans looking for a place to go. When I spoke to Lena, an activist involved in Anti-Fascist Action (AFA) in Göteborg, about Kafé 44, she was obviously enamored with the radical mystique of the café:

My friend lives close to Kafe 44, and I told her that I'd heard about this café and that a lot of radical activist people go there. . . . The first person I see sitting outside is Mattias Wåg. For all the Antifa people, he's like God. . . . I was so shocked at seeing him as the first person in that café. I was sitting there next to him and two guys came in and they looked like normal, seventeen-to-eighteen-year-old guys, but Mattias was like, "They shouldn't be here," and he just stood up and went up to them and said, "Get out," because he thought they were Nazis. [Kafé 44] is more "their [anti-fascists'] place." They can kick people out if they want to.

Seeing an anti-fascist hero throw suspected skinheads out of the café confirmed Lena's beliefs that Kafé 44 was a place for radical activists. She found this impressive, a sign that Kafé 44 was an exclusive club for people who shared her political views.

Most people I interviewed share Lena's views that Kafé 44 is a socially closed activist institution but do not share her view that this is positive. Rasmus, from Göteborg, says, "I tried to go to Kafé 44 one time, and I was stopped at the door like, 'Hey! You can't go in there, it's a separatist party.' And I never tried to go there again. [laughs]" Similarly, Jakob from Stockholm told me that he experienced Kafé 44 as a "closed" place:

> The organization of the café is really closed. It's really hard to get involved there. The place is really bureaucratic. . . . I've tried to get in there and do some things before, but you have to book the place way far in advance. You kinda have to know somebody who works there to get anything done there, which is a bummer.

According to Jakob, the café is "closed" in terms of organization (bureaucratic), time (booking in advance), and social boundaries (knowing someone). Similarly, Tobias in Göteborg says,

> I've heard lots of good stuff about Kafé 44, but it seems like they're a very established place. [. . .] I don't really know much about how they run, but it seems to be like an institution almost. What I've heard, they do really good stuff and they have lots of good happenings there, and when I've been in Stockholm at different happenings, they're always at the center of what's going on, but it's very . . . established.

Tobias uses the words "established" and "institution" to describe the café. While he acknowledges that perhaps they are central to the activist and party scenes in Stockholm, they operate in a more formal fashion than Underjorden, the social center where he worked in Göteborg. Erik, one of the builders from Cyklopen, told me that he found the closed nature of 44 frustrating and that it was something activists from Kulturkampanjen wanted to avoid when building Cyklopen:

When we started Cyklopen, people were reacting to that, to the closed café. [. . .] At 44 you have to jump through a bunch of hoops. You have to wait until they have their consensus meetings. You have to present your idea to the group and then they have to talk about it. They may only have those meetings once a month, so that's a long time. One month to present it and one for them to talk about it, blah blah blah whatever. It's very . . . it just takes all the energy out of it.

Erik contrasts the openness of Cyklopen with the closed nature of Kafé 44. At Cyklopen, all one had to do is show up at the center and ask for a key. At Kafé 44, there is a lengthy decision-making process that Erik sees as overly bureaucratic and unnecessary. This is probably a practical necessity for the volume of requests the café receives, as a popular place that has been operating for more than thirty-five years. But for Erik and others I interviewed, the decision-making processes "take all the energy out" of whatever a person might want to accomplish.

Although Kafé 44 is a radical institution that everyone venerated for its longevity and political history, several activists viewed its decision-making processes as slow and prohibitive of action. By becoming "established" and "an institution," people saw it as an exclusive club for activists rather than a place where new possibilities for action could unfold. Nonetheless, it still served as a reference point as new spaces and places were formed. While contemporary activists rejected the slow, bureaucratic procedures for decision making, they also emulated them in some respects. The "consensus meetings" (stormöte) that Erik mentions are the same kind of decision-making process that social centers use. It is also clear that while activists may find the institutionalization of 44 annoyingly sluggish, they seek to establish similar places themselves.

Stockholm and Göteborg: The Limitations of Squatting

One challenge for scene building in Stockholm and Göteborg is the use of squatting as the primary tactic for attempting to gain access to places.[5] Between 2008 and 2009 there were sixty-five squatting actions throughout Sweden, from Malmö to Umeå, lasting anywhere from one to sixty-two days. A map from the anarchist magazine *Brand* indicates that squatting was more prevalent in Göteborg and Stockholm than in Malmö during this period. My observations from 2009 to 2011 support this as well, as I visited and read about more squatting actions during my time in the two larger cities.

For some people involved in squatting actions, the temporary quality of squats is not a problem because they see it as a symbolic protest tactic geared toward drawing attention to issues of space and place. In a brief essay, Stockholm-based activist Mattias Wåg (2010, 27) writes, "Squats have become short-term, the police raid them within just a few days. But the squatting movement has learned a lesson—you fight for self-managed places, not a specific building." This passage emphasizes the difference between places and buildings, implying that place is a more abstract quality. It also highlights that squatting is not about conservation of buildings, but about a quality of place (self-management). Squatters are not squatting to save buildings but to create a space—temporary or not—for a way of life that is informed by their political beliefs.

Wåg (2010, 27) goes on to write that "it was something more than just squatting for the sake of squatting—it became a way for local society to work together and create resistance." With this statement, Wåg points out that the squatting movement is more than a symbolic movement aimed at preserving a way of life; it was also a means for people to come together and "create resistance" locally. The temporary quality of the squats is not important because the action or process of squatting brings people together. The process of protest is as important as—or perhaps more important than—the outcome of the protests. The possibilities of squatting as a protest tactic became even greater when people considered these actions as a means of diffus-

---

5. For a comprehensive overview on the history of squatting in Sweden, see Polanska (2019).

ing movement ideas. Wåg (2010, 27) continues his essay by writing, "What happens if this method [squatting] spreads again? If squatting suddenly becomes a reasonable action to take when an area is threated by privatization and gentrification or sale of public space. Imagine if everyone began squatting?" Jenny, a squatter in Stockholm, said something similar when she told me about her experience squatting at Aspuddsbadet, a bathhouse in the southern suburb of Aspudden: "Of those who were there from the beginning I'm probably the only one who had squatted before. I think it was a big step for quite a few to go in and occupy a building that was not their own. Now it feels as if that step is much smaller." These musings imagine a future in which squatting becomes a common practice. Jenny points to the beginnings of this at the squat in Aspudden, where most people had not participated in such an action before. She says now that they've done it once, they might not hesitate to do it again, to make it a commonplace way for making demands.

My data suggest that activists squat buildings to draw attention to a lack of available space in cities (political squatting) *and* demand space for social and cultural activities (entrepreneurial squatting). While the people I interviewed saw the points that Wåg makes about the symbolic importance of squatting and its potential for creating connections among activists, none of them viewed squatting as an effective strategy for gaining access to places that social movements could use to develop a cultural scene. Their reasoning was that squatting actions are too short-lived and have little *reach* in terms of establishing a place for themselves in cities.

Rikard, a squatter in Stockholm, said that "you can't really squat to live or to get a place [*lokal*] in Sweden. They just don't last long enough." Similarly, Rasmus in Göteborg says, "There've been lots of things—occupying, trying to occupy houses, but they only last for like two weeks or something [laughs], so it's not really a basis for building up something." Lena had been part of a squatting action in Kviberg, the northeastern part of Göteborg, in March 2010. When I asked how she would describe what went on there, she replied,

There was a room where people were drawing graffiti and playing football and there was another room that was a café, people were reading books. In another room, we showed political films and we had a lot of info tables where Revolutionary Front put their flyers and No One Is Illegal had their flyers there too.

These observations show that the activities of the squat in Kviberg—and most others—mirror the kinds of activities that happen in social center: cafés, libraries, games, circulation of movement ideas. This is similar to a squat that I visited in Liljeholmen, in the southern suburbs of Stockholm. The building had been evacuated by the time I arrived, but signs that the building had been squatted still remained. As I approached, I could see a large banner bearing the international squatters' symbol draped on the side of the building. The front door had the familiar refrain "Sweden ends here" spray-painted across the door in red. On the same door hung a sign that read:

> In this building an occupation is taking place. We are tired of not having anywhere to be and since politicians have consistently refused to help us, we have taken things into our own hands. In the building activities are happening every day, including: workshops, concerts, "people's kitchen," film showings, tattoo studio, art workshops. Please drop by and see how things are going and participate. Everyone is welcome.

In their welcoming statement to visitors, the squatters in Liljeholmen write that they are "tired of not having anywhere to be." Having a place to be is important enough for them to break the law and take over a building, even if it only lasted for five weeks. In other words, having a temporary place to be was better than nothing. The sign on the front of the squat in Liljeholmen is reminiscent of the "Do's and Don'ts" list inside the entrance of Utkanten, the social center in Malmö. Squats are temporary social centers in cities where social movements are not part of the fabric of urban neighborhoods. Squatting a building provides a temporary solution to an ongoing problem.

Rasmus mentions that squats are ineffective for "building up something." The sign on the door refers to "[taking] things into our own hands." When I asked Jenny, a squatter from the house in Liljeholmen about the kinds of rules I had observed at squats and social centers around the country, she said, "Of course we want these spaces to be DIY, but there has to be some kind of rules so that we can actually get some things done rather than just have a big house where people can play." In reference to the squatting action at Kviberg in Göteborg, Lena described "a room where people discussed why they're here and what they think, and how can we develop this action more, how can we actually change something? Instead of just occupying this house, how can we take this further?" These comments speak to the lack of *reach* that squatting actions have for the future. In the present, they allow people to "take things into their own hands," "get things done," and "discuss how to take action further." Taken together, these comments demonstrate that the present is a first step, but activists are thinking about the future. They want to feel as if they have social influence, that what they're doing matters. When a squatting action takes months to plan and then is raided in a few weeks, it deflates their sense of efficacy for shaping their environments, lives, and futures.

The Effects of Fragile and Fledgling Scenes

In Malmö, the temporary character of Right to the City actions prompted activists to look for ways in which they could make their mark on the landscape in an effort to make their scene and movement more durable, showing an orientation toward the future. The differing configurations of the scenes in Stockholm and Göteborg had consequences for both the internal dynamics of the scenes and their potential to affect change in their cities. In terms of internal dynamics, the fragility of the autonomous scene in Stockholm reinforced fleeting relationships and loose networks. If autonomous movements had more visible, central, concentrated places, the relationships, excitement, and affective bonds that were generated during squatting and other direct actions could be sustained, creating momentum for the future. In Göteborg, the concentration of the scene produced exclusivity and inaccessibility, making it difficult for the movement to grow or develop. A wider variety of places that were visible, central, and proximate would, perhaps, increase opportunities for a wider variety of people to become involved in autonomous politics.

These fragile and fledgling scene configurations have different outcomes for social movements and urban neighborhoods than strong scenes. In both Stockholm and Göteborg, the spatial dimensions of the scene had effects on how autonomous activists thought about the future. When people are spread out geographically and identify in a number of different ways, they need a central location where they come together, forge relationships, and hopefully plan actions together. Temporary spaces (anarchist book fair, squats) bring people together but do not last beyond a few days or weeks. Most activists I interviewed in Stockholm and Göteborg are focused on the present and immediate future because the challenges they face in the here and now are most pressing. In Stockholm, the fragility of the scene made finding ways to come together an immediate concern. In Göteborg, the concentration of the scene made finding ways to bring new people into the fold a priority. These immediate concerns took precedent over long-term impact. Again and again, their narratives about the future highlight the importance of place for meeting others, grounding actions, and imagining themselves as having influence on their cities.

Stockholm: Fleeting Relationships and Gemenskap

Social movement scholars acknowledge the importance of collective emotions and affective bonds for reinforcing solidarity among activist groups. In Stockholm, activists talked about the fleeting character of these collective emotions as a negative effect of the fragility of the social movement scene. Activists routinely linked the fleeting character of these emotions to place. While temporary spaces bring people together and create a sense of excitement in the moment, when those spaces disappear, so do the collective emotions. This not only points to the importance of places that have reach into the future but also raises questions about how to maintain the affective bonds and sense of excitement that events and temporary spaces generate.

The concept of *gemenskap* emerged in my interviews as "the emotional energy . . . of people who see themselves as in some way connected" (Gould 2001, 147). This shares many characteristics with Émile Durkheim's ([1912] 1995) concept of "collective effervescence," excitement and emotion that creates a sense of unity among people in social gatherings. Durkheim ([1912] 1995, 218) writes, "The very act of congregating is an exceptionally powerful stimulant. Once the individuals are gathered together, a sort of electricity is generated from their closeness and quickly launches them to an extraordinary height of exaltation." Although Durkheim was writing about religious gatherings, any ritual gathering in which there is a shared focus can generate these feelings of connectedness. During a squatting action or street festival, activists feel the "electricity" that courses through such events. But once the events end, so too does the excitement and feeling of being part of something larger than themselves.

Most activists describe *gemenskap* as a shared emotional bond or "a way of feeling close to other people." Elin, an activist in Stockholm, describes *gemenskap* as "a connection, you feel that you're part of a community. It's like a chain, like you feel like one of the links in the chain all connected together. That's a very visual idea of *gemenskap*." Elin's image of *gemenskap* is one of emotional bonds between people who are individuals, linked together to form a collective. Similarly, Lena describes it as a familial kind of bond: "When you feel *gemenskap*, you feel familiarity, a kind of extended family feeling."

Other narratives point to *gemenskap* as something required to collectively move toward the future. The anarchist publication *Brand* explains that "*gemenskap* emerges when people find one another, when they work together, and collectively decide on a *common path forward*. . . . It is the joy in a meeting that *survives its expected end*" (Anonymous 2010b, 14, emphasis added). This points to the importance of *gemenskap* not only as a sense of collective emotional bonds but also as a collective journey—"a common path forward" in an attempt to keep the collective energy moving toward the future. An interview with Sanna (Anonymous 2010a, 33), a squatter in Stockholm, reveals how many activists I interviewed link *gemenskap* with place:

> INTERVIEWER: The *gemenskap* that emerged during the [squatting action] must have been almost as important as the place. Will that *gemenskap* survive?
> SANNA: I don't think so. *Gemenskap* does not survive without meeting places. It feels so fucking bad. There needs to be something [in this area].

The interviewer comments that a recent squatting created a sense of *gemenskap*, which may be "almost as important as the place" itself.

Sanna disagrees, saying that these shared bonds cannot "survive" without places where they can grow and develop.

One attempt to generate lasting connections among Stockholm activists was the first annual Anarchist Book Fair in June 2010. Activists originally planned the book fair as part of a celebration for the one hundredth anniversary of the Central Organization of the Workers of Sweden (*Sveriges Arbetares Centralorganisation* or SAC), a syndicalist union with anarchist ties. The SAC owns a building in Stockholm where they publish their magazine *Direkt Aktion*, so organizers thought this seemed like a good place and occasion for a book fair. The building needed renovations, so the location fell through, but organizers continued with the idea of the book fair anyway, settling on a location in the southern suburbs called Midsommargården (a social and community center).

As I emerged from the subway station and neared Midsommargården, I began to hear music and in the distance I saw a food tent and a large black banner that read "Anarchist Book Fair" in white lettering. As I approached the building, large groups of people milled around outside, eating and chatting in the sun. Several families were present and their young children ran around in front of the building, laughing and playing. Just inside the entrance was an information table with flyers for an anarchist book fair in London, things to do in Stockholm, city maps, and Stockholm's *Free Paper* (*Fria Tidning*). Upstairs the hallways were lined with tables that were stacked with books, newspapers, glossy magazines, and handmade zines. Writers, editors, publishers, and activists invited passersby to stop and take a look at their publications. In the meeting rooms, there were panels and discussion groups on various topics. I bumped into Mads, one of the fair's organizers, whom I had interviewed several months before. I commented that despite our conversation about the lack of a scene in the city, they had an excellent turnout at the fair. "I know!" he exclaimed. "There are so many people here! Of course they're from all over Sweden and the Baltic region, but . . . maybe this will help get things going around town."

During our conversation some months before, Mads had been critical of the lack of communication between activist groups in Stockholm. He said that "one motivation [for organizing the book fair] was the lack of communication here [in Stockholm] among activist groups." The major goal of the book fair, he said, was to facilitate connections between activist groups who might be geographically separated and/or unknown to one another. At the book fair, I saw many familiar faces: Mathias Wåg, editor of the anarchist magazine *Brand*; staff members from both the INFO bookshop and the café at Kafé 44; activists from Alarm Stockholm; people from Cyklopen; and even a couple of regulars from Glassfabriken in Malmö. If one of the goals of the book fair was to get people from a variety of groups to show up in one place, it was a success.

However, there was not any evidence that the fair helped "get things going around town," as Mads had hoped. It is possible that it fostered *relationships* that could lead to collaborative action in the future, but that was not visible to me. I attended a panel called "What is anarchism? Why is it relevant today?" The panelists talked about anarchism as a set of practices rooted in everyday life, highlighting concrete everyday actions, including creating temporary and permanent spaces and places for people to come together. The variety of opinions in the room about what constituted an anarchist space (open vs. closed, cultural centers vs. service-oriented places, activist-only or public) reinforced what I had observed in the activist community in Stockholm more generally: it comprised a variety of voices, opinions, and backgrounds that did not come together to form anything concrete. While I saw many familiar faces at the Anarchist Book Fair, I did not see any evidence that these people and groups connected or collaborated with one another on anything after that day. The fair brought people together in one place and had the potential to foster collaboration among disparate activist networks in Stockholm and Sweden, but there was no evidence that this actually happened. The *gemenskap* generated by the event was as temporary as the event itself.

Göteborg: Exclusion and Lack of Variety

The concentration of the scene in Göteborg had different outcomes than its counterpart in Stockholm. First, in stark contrast to Stockholm, activist groups in Göteborg were tight-knit, producing an exclusive activist scene that was difficult for outsiders to access. Second, while the Stockholm scene coalesced primarily around a series of temporary spaces and events, the scene in Göteborg revolved around one place: Kulturhuset Underjorden, the social center I discussed in Chapter 3. The social center was difficult to access both socially (due to tight-knit friend groups) and geographically (due to being off the beaten path in a peripheral part of town). Taken together, these elements of concentration created an insular, activist clique without much impact on the community or city.

In Göteborg, people wanted the social center Underjorden to serve as a central hub for bringing people together, which it did—but only to a certain extent and for certain people. Tomas, an activist who worked at the social center, says,

> That's been a big mission for Underjorden also, to get all these people to meet each other. I mean because maybe they're just working in their separate groups, they might feel that they have a lot of differences, but when they meet face-to-face they're actually quite similar and have the same ideas and can get along, even if they choose different ways to do political activism.

Like activists in Stockholm, Tomas points out that places serve an important role in reinforcing relationships among activists. Unlike Stockholm, which lacked durable meeting places after the arson of Cyklopen, Underjorden served to bring groups together. Tomas points out that people "work in their separate groups," which may lead to feelings of isolation. Bringing them together, he notes, helps to dispel the idea that just because groups work on different issues or use different tactics, they do not share common values, instead hoping that they find common ground—literally, in the form of Underjorden.

It was clear upon entering Underjorden, whether during quiet daytime hours or large, raucous post-demonstration parties at night, that not everyone was welcome. One of the founding activist networks was Spatt, an anarcho-punk collective, so the place had a clear punk rock aesthetic. Anyone whose appearance did not fit in was met with suspicion or derision, and/or was simply ignored. In my case, it was the latter. Although I had visited several times and had contacts who worked there, the line that defined me as an outsider never blurred or softened. Although I never mentioned feeling like an outsider at Underjorden, a few interviewees commented on it themselves. Tomas described the exclusionary nature of Underjorden to me with some hesitation:

> I've heard a lot of people who said that they *want* to be involved [at Underjorden], but they don't really know *how*. They want to know about the activist networks, how to get involved with them, and when they come there it's like . . . we who have been there, it's hard for us to see this maybe, but we know each other very well and if new people come who don't look like they really fit in, then people aren't very . . . I mean, it's quite hard to . . . you have to work really hard to get into the place, to get into the community. Some people make it, but they work quite hard for it. The people who aren't maybe that social or don't have a lot of self-confidence might have a hard time getting into it.

Tomas is halting in his explanation of the difficulties that people face when trying to gain access to Underjorden. He identifies the strong ties of people working and having an appearance that "doesn't fit in" as potential barriers for gaining the acceptance of others. He pauses several times and is almost apologetic when he says that the people working at Underjorden are perhaps unable to see how difficult it is for others to feel welcome. In an effort to welcome more people and bolster activist connections, the organizers at Underjorden tried to open up a daily café for people to come hang out, drink coffee, and get to know people. Hanna explains that "because people feel that others at [Underjorden] have a hard attitude toward new people, the café has been a good way to get new people into the place." My observations supported this, as I frequently visited the café for a "people's kitchen" dinner on Sundays, and they were well attended by people who were marginally or not active in social movements. Organizers saw this as a success because it helped to draw people into a social movement environment in an "easy" way that did not require much effort.

However, the café only lasted temporarily, limiting its potential for a number of reasons. Rasmus, another person involved at

Underjorden, explained that they had to close the café for two months over the summer for renovations, which had a negative impact. He continues, "This spring [the café] started to be bigger and bigger and more people started to come, but *then* it was closed for two months and now, it's back to the thing that it was before, where no one knows about it or no one thinks it exists." The lack of continuity once again limits the potential for community building because there is little to no follow-through. Second, Rasmus points out that "no one knows about it," alluding to the importance of visibility and centrality. If the place were in a more central, visible location, more people would know about it.

The example of Underjorden speaks to the fragility of a scene as a *network of places and people*. When a social movement coalesces around one place, if that place closes, the scene falls apart (hence the term "fledgling"). In Malmö, by contrast, the social center Utkanten has existed in multiple locations but was able to persist because it was supported by other people and places that are part of the scene. Part of the problem at Underjorden was limited staffing. Tomas says, "It would be good for the environment in the city if it was a place to go in the summer also. But mainly because it's too few people working and keeping the whole thing running, it doesn't work." This speaks to the small, tight-knit group of people who form the core of the Göteborg scene. When one person takes time off or the place has to close, the scene fragments or falls apart. Like the Anarchist Book Fair, the café at Underjorden was intended to be a place for creating connections among disparate, disconnected individuals and groups in the city in order to inspire collaboration for the future. A tight configuration around a peripheral, underground location and a small group of people contributed to the concentration of the scene in Göteborg.

Conclusion

Creating more resilient autonomous places is important because they give movements further "reach" (Mische 2009, 699) or extension into the future. For Malmö activists, the impetus to create movement places came from a frustration and anxiety about engaging in actions that only had a short-term impact. Their orientation toward the future was shaped by the structural changes happening in the neighborhood, already having established places in the neighborhood of Möllevången, and a tight-knit community that helped foster more long-term planning.

The spatial configurations of scenes in Stockholm and Göteborg were partially shaped by the structural conditions of their respective cities. Neighborhoods with social movement histories gentrified decades ago, leaving social movements without a place—metaphorically and materially—in the larger cities. The dimensions of concentration, centrality, and visibility are lacking in the Stockholm and Göteborg scenes. These elements are important because they foster collaboration and connections among activists and wider audiences and enable social movements to become embedded as part of a neighborhood or area.

Autonomous activists in Stockholm and Göteborg also relied primarily on squatting and singular events to gain access to city space. Squatting is not a viable method for accessing places, and one-off events only last for a day or a week. Although one of the goals of these kinds of actions is to foster relationships and create solidarities that may last into the future, there is little evidence that this is actually the case. Instead, the fragility of the scene in Stockholm reinforces loose-knit networks and a lack of *gemenskap* or collective emotional bonds among activists. The concentration of the scene in Göteborg produces exclusivity and a lack of variety in the scene, limiting the movement's potential for making their mark on the urban landscape.

6

The Future of
Place-Based Movements

Studying social movement scenes reveals how the spatial configurations of social movements play crucial roles in shaping action, relational dynamics, and how activists see possibilities for social change. Operating according to a prefigurative logic, autonomous movements reject traditional ways of "doing politics" and try to create alternative ways of life in their neighborhoods and cities. In Sweden, activists see this as a rejection of "Swedishness," as signified by the slogan "Sweden Ends Here" that I saw spray-painted on the doors of squats throughout the country. At the same time, activists draw on the traditions of the Old Left because they see early labor movements as a unique and important part of Swedish history. Place making—"the material, practical, and symbolic construction of place" (Paulsen 2004, 244)—is an important part of their efforts because it gives movements a sense of continuity and resilience. By staking territorial claims on urban space, activists see themselves as creating the basis for a movement that has lasting effects on the future of everyday life.

Place is more than a stage where action unfolds; it is "a structure that guides actions (Giddens, 1984), making some [actions] more or less likely than others" (Paulsen 2004, 259; see also Pred 1984). For autonomous movements, place making is not only a means to an end but an important process in its own right. The social center Cyklopen is an excellent example of how the process of making places is an important goal in itself. The building process was meaningful to people because they learned new skills, built relationships, and exchanged information. The goal of Cyklopen was not only to build a free space where "real" activism could take place. Activist-builders saw the building process as equally important because they were "building the future" by carving out space for themselves in the urban landscape—culturally, politically, and geographically.

Scene places are also important for relationship building among activists. Activists in Malmö described increased collaboration and connection among people as they built new social movement places, crossing the divide between "political" and "cultural" approaches to activism. In Göteborg, autonomous activists attribute the close working relationships they developed at Underjorden as an important reason for seeking out more places in the city that could bring people together. Similarly, activists in Stockholm felt that more social movement places would benefit activist networks by serving as points of connection for the loosely knit community in the city.

The unique spatial configurations of social movement scenes have effects for how, when, and where solidarities are produced. The solidarities among activists in Möllevången/Malmö were not a product of simply living in the same city or neighborhood. The proximity, centrality, and visibility of the scene ensured consistent, frequent contact among people, promoting greater collaboration and cooperation on projects. Their embeddedness in the neighborhood also enabled activists to diffuse the norms and practices of the movement into the neighborhood more broadly. In Göteborg and Stockholm, where scenes are more diffuse and peripheral, they did not have as much influence.

What Do Scenes Do for Social Movements?

This study suggests that scenes are important for social movement momentum and vitality. The concept of a scene connotes malleability, flux, and flow (Stahl 2004). This fluidity is part of what appeals to activists as they create their own spaces and places. The flexibility of scenes gives activists a sense of hope that they can create alternatives for living, working, and relating to others. At the same time, the contingency of these spaces creates a desire for a sense of durability and continuity, a sense that what they are doing matters. While strong scenes and movement places lend autonomous movements a sense of resilience, this does not make them permanent. These places "*seem* durable to the people who recognize and experience them, but they are nonetheless constantly being recreated and subtly changed" (Pierce, Martin and Murphy 2010, 58). In this way, scenes lend social movements a sense of multiple possibilities for the future but also ground their work in ways that makes what they do seem meaningful and durable.

Social movement scholarship primarily focuses on the functions of scenes for social movements without considering how the spatial configurations of these structures affect urban landscapes. My research highlights the importance of widening the lens around activism, zooming out to examine how movements are socially, culturally, and geographically situated in their local environments. Based on a case study of the autonomous scene in Hamburg, Germany, Darcy Leach and Sebastian Haunss (2009, 272) suggest that "due to the greater density of social ties, geographically concentrated scenes . . . are likely to generate more insular norms of interaction and discourse, limiting their scope of influence." My data on Malmö show the opposite effect; dense social networks and geographic concentration enabled activists to *expand* their influence in the neighborhood. It was not only geographic concentration that made this possible but also a combination of other factors, such as changes in the neighborhood that made their message welcome to the public and tactical innovations that enabled broad participation. This underscores the importance of looking at social movements and scenes as part of broader contexts and how changes in the local environment shape and are shaped by activism.

Social movement scenes—social centers in particular—serve as laboratories where autonomous activists practice prefigurative politics. These places can be the foundation for diffusing the ideas fomented in those spaces into neighborhoods and cities more broadly as they were in Malmö. Alternatively, these places can become insular activist cliques—as they did in Göteborg. In that case, autonomous movement scenes might have little effect on society today but still serve as important repositories of social movement norms, cultures, and histories that could become influential in the future (Whittier 1995). This study supports the idea of scenes as "retreat structures" (Leach and Haunss 2009) where activists or people interested in activism can maintain contact with social movements with little to no commitment. Leach and Haunss (2009) write about this in terms of people who get burned out after a long period of activism. Scenes offer people a way to stay involved following a period of intense commitment to protest without necessarily requiring a lot of time or effort. As I described in Chapter 2, some activists view scenes as "a little break from the capitalist world," so I suggest that we can also think of scenes as "retreat structures" in relation to other social structures, such as capitalism or electoral politics. For some people, simply participating in everyday life within scenes is a "retreat" from the social structures of which they are critical. These have important consequences for longevity because scenes provide easy ways for current activists to maintain participation over long periods of time and opens easy paths to activism for people new to movements.

How Are Social Movements Shaped by Urban Environments?

Comparisons of social movement scenes in three cities highlight how structural changes in cities influence the development of social movements and scenes over time. Autonomous networks are forced to leave inner-city neighborhoods as these areas gentrify and become increasingly expensive. Sometimes this takes the form of direct expulsion, such as when the landlord of the social center Utkanten did not renew their lease or when police raid squatted buildings. At other times these moves are more indirect, such as when rents become too high for activist networks to sustain, as was the case with the social center Underjorden in Göteborg. In Möllevången/Malmö, infrastructural, demographic, and cultural changes affecting the neighborhood provided the impetus for Right to the City movements. Their actions were motivated by fears about social movements losing their place in the neighborhood and thus created more scene places in an attempt to solidify their place in Möllevången. In Stockholm and Göteborg, social movements were priced out of analogous neighborhoods decades ago, making their movements—and scenes—more scattered and disconnected as they seek to find their place.

How Do Social Movements Affect Change in the Urban Landscape?

Many Right to the City campaigns (in Sweden and elsewhere) coalesce around issues related to gentrification processes: changes in housing tenure, the influx of upscale commercial businesses, displacement of working-class residents, and increasing commercialization of city centers. However, literature on gentrification rarely focuses attention on groups that oppose these changes, instead focusing on displacement of individuals as victims of gentrification (Betancur 2011; Newman and Wyly 2006; Pérez 2004) or on middle-class gentrifiers (Brown-Saracino 2009).

My research shows that social movements are important collective actors in the gentrification process and that activists often occupy dual positions as both gentrifiers and displaced residents. On one hand, autonomous movements bring cultural vitality to neighborhoods in the form of public art, music shows, protests, and other cultural activities. This contributes to creating a "buzz" in a neighborhood that makes it attractive to others. Activists in Malmö recognized themselves as part of the gentrification process because the Möllevång Festival contributed to the image of their neighborhood as a desirable place to be. On the other hand, the more desirable the neighborhood becomes, the less affordable it becomes for living or doing activism.

Attention to the spatial dynamics of social movement scenes also shows how social movements carve out space in the urban landscape, whether temporarily or permanently (or somewhere in between). Movement action is shaped by the local environment, but social movements also shape the landscapes of which they are a part. In Malmö, organizers of the Möllevång Festival changed the landscape by turning the streets into an extension of people's living rooms. In doing so, they made the social interactions of neighbors central instead of traffic. Extending the living rooms of residents into the streets can have reverberating effects in shaping the character of public life in the neighborhood. In this way, they shaped not only the physical landscape but the social landscape of the neighborhood as well.

How Do the Spatial Aspects of Social Movements Shape Activists' Visions for the Future?

The scene in Malmö highlights the interplay between structure and agency as a means of creating possibilities for the future. As infrastructural, demographic, and cultural changes unfolded in Möllevången/Malmö (structure), social movements were constrained by rules and regulations, evictions, and lack of resources but enabled by a changing social context that helped them appeal to a broad audience. As they engaged in projects aimed at the right to the city, activists diffused the ideas, norms, and practices to the neighborhood more broadly (action). In turn, this helped them create more places in the neighborhood to serve as a structural basis for future actions.

This understanding of agency is intimately linked with the temporal orientations of activist groups (Blee 2012) and places. The linkage of the past, present, and future is a thread that runs through activist narratives about place making and movement vitality. In these narratives, they "reconstruct their view of the past in an attempt to understand the causal conditioning of the emergent present, while using this understanding to control and shape their responses in the arising future" (Emirbayer and Mische 1998, 966; see also Blee 2012). In Stockholm, Göteborg, and Malmö, activists drew upon the past as they created scene places, citing the culture of the labor movement and People's Houses as sources of inspiration for their own efforts. Part of what they found appealing about that cultural history was its emphasis on self-management and freedom from the state. Activists talked about welfare retrenchment, for example, as a reason to "stir things up collectively" in the present and create a more secure future for themselves without relying on the state. A problem cited by activists in all three cities was that occupying temporary spaces, such the Anarchist Book Fair or the Möllevång Festival, had temporary effects. Part of the appeal of a brick-and-mortar manifestation of their goals was that it lends their movements, goals, and visions a greater sense of resilience.

Whether or not imagined futures actually come true, they do shape action (Blee 2012; Mische 2009). My research suggests that spatial dynamics are crucial in these processes. Place making shapes how activists think about the future, which then impacts their actions. The resulting "cascading sequences of actions" have important consequences because they form the paths that activist groups take in their efforts to create social change (Blee 2012, 35). The paths that activists take may "stifle the range of possibilities they consider," (Blee 2012, 136) as is the case in Stockholm and Göteborg, where activists rely primarily on squatting as a means of accessing places, despite its ineffectiveness. On the other hand, activists sometimes shake up their usual routines, like the activists at Cyklopen who broke the mold for autonomous movements all over Sweden.

With the emphasis on space and place, my study highlights three dimensions of futurity—reach, contingency, and volition. Activists viewed place making as an important way of creating *reach* or the extension of movement goals and priorities into the future. An emphasis on reach was about creating longevity not only for a particular place but also for what those places represented: visions, goals, and dreams for how society could be in the future.

Contingency refers to "the degree to which future trajectories are imagined as fixed and predetermined versus flexible, uncertain and dependent on local circumstances" (Mische 2009, 700). Activists in Malmö talked about the march of gentrification as an inevitable process of change but demanded to be part of the decision-making processes regarding how city space was used and by whom. Their view of the future as inevitable shaped how they responded to these changes. They did not claim to want to *stop* the processes in the neighborhood, but they did seek to intervene and become part of the conversation. Activists at Cyklopen, on the other hand, saw the future as much more contingent, given the unpredictable circumstances they encountered when their first social center became the target of arson. A series of "cascading events and actions" (Blee 2012, 33), such as the arson, support from unlikely sources, and an increase in resources and expertise, allowed activists at Cyklopen to see the future as open to all kinds of possibilities for change.

The dimension of contingency is linked to *volition*, the "motion or influence that the actor holds in regard to the impending future"

(Mische 2009, 701). If a group sees the future as inevitable or predetermined, they may likely feel as if they have less influence over that future. This may explain why activists in Malmö sought to become an embedded part of the community via establishing places in the neighborhood. Since they saw the future as marching toward them, they sought paths for establishing themselves as part of the neighborhood via securing more places in that neighborhood. Activists at Cyklopen, on the other hand, saw the future as more malleable and uncertain. Given the great odds that they overcame in realizing a place that represented their visions for the future, they felt a greater sense of volition. As unlikely events unfolded in the creation of Cyklopen 2.0, activists felt a greater sense of possibilities for social change that were grounded in the place that they created collectively.

Future Research

This study leaves open several avenues for future research on scenes, space and place, and the future. Because scenes are contingent, fluid, and always changing, one path for future research is how scenes change over time. Scholars have begun to theorize the growth, disruption, and decline of scenes and free spaces (Culton and Holtzman 2010), but little is known about the lifecycle of scenes. Where do scenes originate? Under what conditions do fragile scenes become strong or vice versa? What happens when scenes decline? Can scenes die or do they morph into something else? What effect does the lifecycle of a scene have for a movement or neighborhood? What are the causal factors that shape various scene configurations?

Second, scene scholars might engage with questions of scale. Are scenes strictly local phenomena or is there such a thing as a national scene or even a transnational scene? For example, does the network of squats in Europe constitute a sort of continental scene?

Third, I suggest more focus on the relationship between futurity and action. How people imagine the future has an effect on what they do, which, in turn, impacts the series of events that unfold from those actions. More research that investigates these processes would allow sociologists to see a host of internal group dynamics (how groups form, change their course of action, fizzle out) that might otherwise be invisible (Blee 2012). Futurity studies that attend to questions of place, as well, can illuminate how communities can both shape and be shaped by these actions.

A final set of future research questions emerges when considering the importance of space and place for social movements. "The right to the city" is a slogan used by social movements throughout the world, yet little empirical research has examined how movements use this slogan and to what ends. The right to the city refers to "changing the city more after our heart's desire" (Harvey 2003, 941), a vision of the future. Studying how, when, and where social movements use this slogan can show us how people envision the future and how and to what extent their visions are constrained or enabled by their local environments. Scholarship on the right to the city is dominated by political economy theory (Harvey 2003; Purcell 2002, 2008) and would benefit from more cultural analysis. When people make a claim about their city or neighborhood, they are making claims not only on improved material conditions but also on the kind of everyday life they want to preserve or enable. Moreover, some research suggests that the "virtualization" of social movements has important consequences for their spatial and temporal dimensions (van Stekelenburg and Roggeband 2013). How might the importance of place be affected by the "virtualization" of movements? What kinds of interactions exist between virtual and real-world movement spaces (Gerbaudo 2012; Simi and Futrell 2010)?

In 2011, movements throughout the world took to the streets, parks, and plazas of their cities—aided, in part, by virtual communities (Gerbaudo 2012). Occupy protests, the Indignados of Spain, and the Arab Spring uprisings demonstrate that space, place, and territoriality matter for social movements. These movements drew much attention to the politics of public space (Castañeda 2012; Dahliwal 2012; Rabbat 2012; Sassen 2011; Shiffman et al. 2012), highlighting the ways in which the intricacies of place shape and are shaped by social movement action. Movements such as these bring space and place to the center of analysis, raising new questions and debates about the relationship between place and democracy.

Appendix

Methods and Access

Methods

Interviews and ethnographic observations capture the social dynamics of scenes in this book, while *comparative case analysis* reveals some of the driving factors for why scenes thrive or fizzle in different urban environments. Comparative case studies allow us to see "how similar processes lead to different outcomes" in different settings and locales (Bartlett and Vavrus 2016, 15). Like ethnography, comparative case approaches require a high degree of flexibility and iteration. I began this research in Stockholm and Göteborg because they are Sweden's largest cities and appeared (from internet sources) to have active scenes. Even after months of comparing these two cities, my comparative angle was still not immediately clear. It was not until I heard about Malmö from my participants that I visited there and began to understand the general relationships between neighborhoods, movements, and scenes. Going back and forth among cities made these relationships even more clear: differing configurations of social movement scenes are partially shaped by the structural conditions of the cities in which they form. This phased, processual approach to comparison requires researchers to "follow the inquiry in an iterative, emergent research design" (Bartlett and Vavrus 2016, 7; see also Maxwell 2013).

In addition to comparison, this study is based on fourteen months of observation of scene places, content analysis of ephemera produced by activist groups, and in-depth semistructured interviews with thirty-eight people who were active members of autonomous groups in Sweden. All interviewees were Swedish or "Swenglish," with the exception of three people, who came from

Austria, Belgium, and the United States but had five or more years of involvement autonomous places in Sweden. They self-identified in a number of ways: as anarchists, squatters, anti-fascists, feminists, or more often, simply activists or artists—or some combination thereof. What all of them had in common was that they played active roles in autonomous places and spaces. I conducted interviews in English and "Swenglish," a combination of Swedish and English. I gave all Swedish interviewees the option to speak Swedish, and in a few cases, they took me up on the offer, speaking only Swedish with me. In those cases, I asked questions in English and they responded in Swedish so that both of us could clearly express ourselves and neither of us had a linguistic advantage (Marschan-Piekkari and Reis 2004). Most interviewees elected to speak English with me but often switched to Swedish during portions of the interview to express themselves more clearly. I spoke English with the three international interviewees. Communicating with participants in Swedish and/or Swenglish was important for three reasons: it allowed interviewees to express themselves fully, helped me establish rapport, and enabled me to interpret their words in cultural and/or linguistic contexts (Tsang 1998).

Each interview took place in a location chosen by the interviewee. We met in cafés, libraries, social centers, and, in a few cases, in participants' homes. I began each interview with questions aimed at getting a broad picture of the activist scene in each city, such as asking people to describe the scenes in their city and about their own involvement in those scenes. Most often, interviewees worked in a scene place or were part of one or more activist networks, so I asked questions particular to those places and networks. For example, while interviewing someone who worked in a social center, I asked questions about how the center operated, the degree of "openness" of the center (i.e., who was welcome there), how the social center fit into the surrounding community, the relationship of the center with other scene places, and whether they had experienced any conflicts, either internally or with authorities or neighbors. Inevitably these questions led to discussions about urban space; these interviews took place during the "squatting wave," so urban politics were on the minds of many activists. I asked them why squatting and battles over space had taken on renewed importance in Sweden at this particular time, and I elicited specific examples of changes in cities that affected their everyday lives.

There is very little scholarly literature on autonomous movements in Sweden, so I spent a good deal of time collecting historical and contemporary documents to compose a comprehensive history of radical social movements in Sweden. I gathered historical data on radical left-wing movements in Sweden by looking at back issues of the anarchist newspaper *Brand*, the longest-running anarchist newspaper (now a magazine) in the world; all back issues are housed at the Undergraduate and Newspaper Library at Göteborg University.

I conducted comprehensive searches of major newspapers, including *Dagens Nyheter*, *Göteborgs-Posten*, *Svenska Dagbladet*, and *Sydsvenskan*. For all information that was more than three to four years old, I searched microfilm at the Undergraduate and Newspaper Library at Göteborg University. For more recent information, I searched these newspapers via their websites. These searches resulted in more than one hundred articles on urban protests, including squatting, since 1969 (the year of the first squatting protest in Sweden), as well as articles on specific scene places. These sources were valuable not only for tracing the history of radical leftist culture since 1969 but also for gathering public interviews with activists and developing a picture of how autonomous actors and spaces are portrayed by the media and regarded by local authorities and politicians. In interviews, activists often talked about how they had been negatively portrayed by journalists and politicians—which sometimes made them suspicious of me as an interviewer, initially—and looking at news articles helped contextualize the stories and events about which they spoke in interviews and informal conversations.

I also performed content analyses of hundreds of pieces of activist-produced media, including zines (independent, handmade publications), newspapers, flyers, brochures, manifestos, stickers, and books. Three sources have been particularly useful for gathering public interviews and information about events, meetings, demonstrations, and groups to contact: *Brand*, already mentioned; *Direkt Aktion*, a quarterly magazine produced by the Syndicalist Youth Union (Syndikalistisk Ungdomsförbundet) since 1996, and the website Motkraft, a comprehensive source of "news from and about the extraparliamentary left" (motkraft.net).

Notes on Gaining Access

A frequently asked question from people to whom I present my work is "how did you—an American, an academic—get autonomous activists in Sweden to talk to you?" Embedded in this question are a couple of (true) assumptions. First, autonomous movements are notoriously "closed" to outsiders. As an American, I was a cultural and linguistic outsider. Second, autonomous movements can be hostile to academics or fearful of what "insider" information academics might report publicly.

I remained a cultural outsider during my fieldwork for three reasons: I am an academic. I am an American. I am not a native Swedish speaker. Gaining access to networks of activists was extremely difficult for several reasons, not least of which is that scenes are not formally organized entities. Emails to scene places often went unanswered, and getting contact information for individuals was nearly impossible. Because of concerns about privacy of information, many contacts said, "I will ask my friends if they'll talk to you," but would not divulge their friends' contact information, leaving me unable to have any control over whom they asked to participate, when, or how. In a couple of cases, logistics prevented me from being able to get in touch with people who *were* willing to let me interview them. In one instance, I emailed a bookshop and followed up by visiting in person. The woman working said, "Oh yes, there were two people who said they would talk to you, but of course I can't give you their contact information, so please write your phone number down for me to give to them again." Despite my persistent follow-up visits and emails, I never made contact with the two potential interviewees.

As I tried to track down interviewees, I posted a message to an autonomous activist message board to ask if anyone would be willing to participate in my research. One response to my message summarized what a lot people said to me in the course of my fieldwork (though generally in a more polite way): "We don't want to be material for your study." In other cases, people did want to participate but quizzed me on my own background before agreeing to do so. For example, Lena, a young woman involved in Anti-Fascist Action (AFA) wrote to me,

> I would like to be interviewed but first can you tell me more about yourself? What kind of activism have you done? How old are you? Where are you from? My friends say that you might be a cop, so I shouldn't talk to you, but . . . I don't know, I just have a good feeling about you.

Her comment that "my friends say that you might be a cop" shows the suspicion and fear of authorities that groups like AFA cultivate in their members. Lena's reticence continued when we met for the interview. She insisted we meet in a public but hidden place, so we met in the basement of a large library for her interview. Later that summer, she texted me at a music festival, "Hi! I see you here at this music festival, but don't want to say hi because I'm with people from AFA and I don't want them to know you interviewed me." Even after participating in this research, Lena did not want anyone to know that she had, making confidentiality in the field very important.

Not all of my interactions were so clandestine. I found "gatekeepers" through a variety of channels: by asking Swedish social movement scholars for interview contacts, by emailing activist networks and scene places, and by telling everyone I met about my project and my need for contacts. When I attended an event or showed up to a scene location with a known activist, I was welcomed and people graciously answered questions and asked questions about me, but I still remained an outsider, both culturally and socially.

Elin, an activist in Malmö, pointed out that I might have trouble getting access because I am American. She said, "For better or worse, there are a lot of negative things associated with being American, so I'm sorry to say that that might be a reason why people—especially anti-capitalists—don't want to talk to you." "Wow," I said, "I've never heard that before. Usually people just say, 'I don't want to talk to you because you're a researcher.'" "Well . . . that's easier to say," she replied.

Another difficulty was that in Sweden, strangers just don't talk to one another, even in the most public of spaces. When I told a Swedish acquaintance about my plan to simply approach people in public spaces to ask questions as an observer, she looked horrified. "You can't do that here," she said. "People will think you're crazy." She went on to say, "People say that if you talk to someone you don't know in public, you must be drunk, crazy, or American." Unfortunately, she was right. Approaching people in cafés or bookshops to strike up an informal conversation or ask even basic questions raised suspicions, particularly among activists, about who I was and what I wanted to know.

Often, I found myself being a more passive participant than I would have been had I been in a similar situation in the United States because I was self-conscious about my language skills or did not think that I could effectively communicate what I wanted to say in Swedish. This was especially true at the beginning of my fieldwork when I was getting my footing in a new culture. At times my Swedish, while fine for everyday conversation and one-on-one interviews, made it difficult to keep up with group conversations. While I understood everything people were saying, at times it was difficult to express myself under the pressure of several people staring at me.

Being an outsider was not always disadvantageous; sometimes being an English speaker allowed me to see and hear things that insiders might take for granted. Since I am not a native Swedish speaker, I became very attuned to language and word choice, which sometimes revealed important analytical points. For example, in Malmö, I noticed that people used different terms to refer to city residents (*Malmöbor*) and residents of the neighborhood Möllevången (*Möllevångare*). As I describe in Chapter 4, this linguistic convention marks the neighborhood and its residents as special.

While I was a cultural outsider in some respects, I was also a cultural insider in ways that allowed me to build rapport with participants. As a white woman in my thirties with experience in feminist and queer activism and DIY punk rock cultures, I resembled many of the people I interviewed. Most participants assumed that my interest in them implied some kind of activist history. Upon my initial meetings with people, I was often asked, "What kind of activism have you done?" and I answered honestly. I do not identify as anarchist or autonomous, but my involvement in feminist and queer politics allowed people to connect with me—and often reassured those who were suspicious about my motives.

Bibliography

Adinolfi, Martina. 2019. "The Squatting Effect: From Urban Removal to Urban Renewal." In *Where Is Europe? Respacing, Replacing, Reordering Europe*, edited by Janny de Jong, Marek Neuman, and Margriet van der Waal, 48–61. Groningen, Netherlands: Euroculture Consortium. https://www.rug.nl /research/portal/files/91102375/Where_is_Europe.pdf#page=56.

Adkins, Lisa. 2009. "Sociological Futures: From Clock Time to Event Time." *Sociological Research Online* 14 (4): 88–92. https://doi.org/10.5153/sro.1976.

Agius, C. 2006. "Sweden's 2006 Parliamentary Election and After: Contesting or Consolidating the Swedish Model?" *Parliamentary Affairs* 60 (4): 585–600. https://doi.org/10.1093/pa/gsm041.

Aguilera, Thomas. 2018. "The Squatting Movement(s) in Paris: Internal Divides and Conditions for Its Survival." In *The Urban Politics of Squatters' Movements*, edited by Miguel Martínez López, 121–144. London: Palgrave Macmillan.

Alarm Stockholm. 2007a. "Stockholm är Förstört." http://alarmsthlm.com/2007 /11/20/stockholm-ar-forstort/.

———. 2007b. "Vi Vill Ha en Stad för Alla." http://alarmsthlm.com/2008/11/12 /vi-vill-ha-en-stad-for-alla/.

Allen, Shaonta', and Brittney Miles. 2020. "Unapologetic Blackness in Action: Embodied Resistance and Social Movement Scenes in Black Celebrity Activism." *Humanity and Society* 44 (4): 375–402.

Allt åt Alla. 2014. "Staden på Tvären—Stadskamp i Södra Förorterna." http:// alltatalla.com/stockholm/staden-pa-tvaren-%E2%80%93-stadskamp-i -sodra-fororterna.

Amnå, Erik. 2006a. "Associational Life, Youth, and Political Capital Formation in Sweden: Historical Legacies and Contemporary Trends." In *State and Civil Society in Northern Europe: The Swedish Model Reconsidered*, edited by Lars Trägårdh, 165–204. New York: Berghahn Books.

———. 2006b. "Playing with Fire? Swedish Mobilization for Participatory Democracy." *Journal of European Public Policy* 13 (4): 587–606. https://doi.org /10.1080/13501760600693952.

Anarkistiska Studier. 2008. "Anarkism: Organisering." Booklet.

Anderson, Ben, and Colin McFarlane. 2011. "Assemblage and Geography." *Area* 43: 124–127. http://dx.doi.org/10.1111/j.1475-4762.2011.01004.x.

Andersson, Jenny. 2009. "Nordic Nostalgia and Nordic Light: The Swedish Model as Utopia 1930–2007." *Scandinavian Journal of History* 34 (3): 229–245. https://doi.org/10.1080/03468750903134699.

Andersson, Roger, and Lena Magnusson Turner. 2014. "Segregation, Gentrification, and Residualisation: From Public Housing to Market-Driven Housing Allocation in Inner City Stockholm." *International Journal of Housing Policy* 14 (1): 3–29. https://doi.org/10.1080/14616718.2013.872949.

Anjou, Mikael. 2011. "Stad Solidar Rivs." *Sydsvenskan*, February 11. http://www .sydsvenskan.se/malmo/stad-solidar-rivs/.

Annunziata, Sandra, and Clara Rivas-Alonso. 2020. "Everyday Resistances in Gentrifying Contexts." In *Resistances: Between Theories and the Field*, edited by Sarah Murru and Abel Polese, 61–82. London: Rowman and Littlefield.

Anonymous. 2008. "Swedish Anarchists Build Their Own Autonomous Zone." *Rolling Thunder* 6: 42–56.

———. 2010a. "Aspuddsbadet." *Brand* 1: 32–33.

———. 2010b. "G som i Gemenskap." *Brand* 1: 14–15.

Arampatzi, Athina. 2017. "The Spatiality of Counter-Austerity Politics in Athens, Greece: Emergent 'Urban Solidarity Spaces.'" *Urban Studies* 54 (9): 2155–2171. https://doi.org/10.1177/0042098016629311.

Ariadad, Samira, and Rasmus Fleischer. 2010. "Att Göra Gemensamma Rum." *Brand* 1: 45–46.

Attoh, Kafui. 2011. "What Kind of Right Is the Right to the City?" *Progress in Human Geography* 35 (5): 669–685. https://doi.org/10.1177/0309132510394706.

Baeten, Guy, Sara Westin, Emil Pull, and Irene Molina. 2017. "Pressure and Violence: Housing Renovation and Displacement in Sweden." *Environment and Planning A: Economy and Space* 49 (3): 631–651.

Bartlett, Lesley, and Frances Vavrus. 2016. *Rethinking Case Study Research: A Comparative Approach*. New York: Routledge. https://doi.org/10.4324 /9781315674889.

BDS Sweden. 2014. "Isolera Israel." https://www.facebook.com/isoleraisrael/.

Bengtsson, Halfdan. 1938. "The Temperance Movement and Temperance Legislation in Sweden." *Annals of the American Academy of Political and Social Science* 197: 134–153.

Bennett, Andy, and Keith Kahn-Harris, eds. 2004. *After Subculture: Critical Studies in Contemporary Youth Culture.* New York: Palgrave Macmillan.

Bennett, Andy, and Richard A. Peterson. 2004. *Music Scenes: Local, Translocal, and Virtual.* Nashville, TN: Vanderbilt University Press.

"Berättelser om Cyklopen." 2012. http://www.cyklopen.se/detta-ar-cyklopen /berattelser-om-cyklopen/.

Bergbom, Kalle, and Fredrik Öjemar. 2008. "Branden på Cyklopen Var Anlagd." *Dagens Nyheter,* December 1. http://www.dn.se/sthlm/branden-pa -cyklopen-var-anlagd%5C.

Berglund, Karin. 1988. "Husnallarna ger inte upp." *Dagens Nyheter,* January 20, 1988.

Betancur, John. 2011. "Gentrification and Community Fabric in Chicago." *Urban Studies* 48 (2): 383–406. https://doi.org/ doi.org/0.1177/0042098 009360680.

Blee, Kathleen. 2012. *Democracy in the Making: How Activist Groups Form.* New York: Oxford University Press.

———. 2013. "How Options Disappear: Causality and Emergence in Grassroots Activist Groups." *American Journal of Sociology* 119 (3): 655–681. https:// doi.org/10.1086/675347.

Borg, Kristian. 2013. "Cyklopen Bygger Framtidens Politik." *Stockholms Fria,* September 20. http://www.fria.nu/artikel/112092.

Brown-Saracino, Japonica. 2009. *A Neighborhood That Never Changes: Gentrification, Social Preservation, and the Search for Authenticity.* Chicago: University of Chicago Press.

Bryson, Jeremy. 2013. "The Nature of Gentrification." *Geography Compass* 7 (8): 578–587. https://doi.org/10.1111/gec3.12056.

Castañeda, Ernesto. 2012. "The Indignados of Spain: A Precedent to Occupy Wall Street." *Social Movement Studies* 11 (3–4): 309–319. https://doi.org/10 .1080/14742837.2012.708830.

Castell, Pål, Sara Danielsson, and Ilona Stehn. 2008. "Staden Är Ditt Vardagsrum." *Fria Tidningen,* November 26. https://www.fria.nu/artikel/76114.

Chatterton, Paul. 2010. "So What Does It Mean to Be an Anti-Capitalist? Conversations with Activists in Urban Social Centres." *Urban Studies* 47 (6): 1205–1224. https://doi.org/10.1177/0042098009360222.

Christophers, Brett. 2013. "A Monstrous Hybrid: The Political Economy of Housing in Twenty-First Century Sweden." *New Political Economy* 18 (6): 885–911.

Collins, Randall. 2004. *Interaction Ritual Chains.* Princeton, NJ: Princeton University Press.

Cornish, Flora, Jan Haaken, Liora Moskovitz, and Sharon Jackson. 2016. "Rethinking Prefigurative Politics: Introduction to the Special Thematic Section." *Journal of Social and Political Psychology* 4 (1): 114–127. https://doi.org /10.5964/jspp.v4i1.640.

Couto, Richard. 1993. "Narrative, Free Space, and Political Leadership in Social Movements." *Journal of Politics* 55 (1): 57–79.

Creasap, Kimberly. 2012. "Social Movement Scenes: Place-Based Politics and Everyday Resistance." *Sociology Compass* 6 (2): 182–191. https://doi.org/10.2307/2132228.

———. 2016. "Finding the Movement: The Geographies of Social Movement Scenes." *International Journal of Sociology and Social Policy* 36 (11/12): 792–807. https://doi.org/10.1108/IJSSP-11-2015-0130.

———. 2020. "'Building Future Politics': Projectivity and Prefiguration in a Swedish Social Center." *Social Movement Studies*, July 28. https://doi.org/10.1080/14742837.2020.1798752.

Culton, Kenneth R., and Ben Holtzman. 2010. "The Growth and Disruption of a 'Free Space': Examining a Suburban Do It Yourself (DIY) Punk Scene." *Space and Culture* 13 (3): 270–284. https://doi.org/10.1177/1206331210365258.

Dahliwal, Puneet. 2012. "Public Squares and Resistance: The Politics of Space in the Indignados Movement." *Interface: A Journal for and about Social Movements* 4 (1): 251–273.

Davidson, Mark, and Loretta Lees. 2010. "New-Build Gentrification: Its Histories, Trajectories, and Critical Geographies." *Population, Space and Place* 16 (5): 395–411. https://doi.org/10.1002/psp.584.

Davies, Andrew D. 2012. "Assemblage and Social Movements: Tibet Support Groups and the Spatialities of Political Organisation." *Transactions of the Institute of British Geographers* 37 (2): 273–286.

De Backer, Mattias. 2019. "Regimes of Visibility: Hanging Out in Brussels' Public Spaces." *Space and Culture* 22 (3): 308–320. https://doi.org/10.1177/1206331218773292.

Deleuze, Gilles, and Felix Guattari. 1987. *A Thousand Plateaus: Capitalism and Schizophrenia*. Minneapolis: University of Minnesota Press.

Della Porta, Donatella, and Mario Diani. 2006. *Social Movements: An Introduction*. Malden, MA: Blackwell.

Domaradzka, Anna. 2018. "Urban Social Movements and the Right to the City: An Introduction to the Special Issue on Urban Mobilization." VOLUNTAS: *International Journal of Voluntary and Nonprofit Organizations* 29 (4): 607–620. https://doi.org/10.1007/s11266-018-0030-y.

Durkheim, Émile. (1912) 1995. *The Elementary Forms of Religious Life*. New York: Free Press.

Edling, Niels. 2019. "The Languages of Welfare in Sweden." In *Changing Meanings of the Welfare State: Histories of a Key Concept in the Nordic Countries*, edited by Niels Edling, 76–136. New York: Berghahn Books.

Emirbayer, Mustafa, and Ann Mische. 1998. "What Is Agency?" *American Journal of Sociology* 103 (4): 962–1023. https://doi.org/10.1086/231294.

Enke, Anne. 2007. *Finding the Movement: Sexuality, Contested Space and Feminist Activism*. Durham, NC: Duke University Press.

Evans, Sara M., and Harry C. Boyte. 1992. *Free Spaces: The Sources of Democratic Change in America*. Chicago: University of Chicago Press.

Falkheimer, Jesper. 2016. "Place Branding in the Øresund Region: From a Transnational Region to a Bi-national City-Region." *Place Branding and Public Diplomacy* 12: 160–171. https://doi.org/10.1057/s41254-016-0012-z.

Fantasia, Rick, and Eric L. Hirsch. 1995. "Culture in Rebellion: The Appropriation and Transformation of the Veil in the Algerian Revolution." In *Social Movements and Culture*, edited by Hank Johnston and Bert Klandermans, 144–160. Minneapolis: University of Minnesota Press.

Florida, Richard L. 2002. *The Rise of the Creative Class: And How It's Transforming Work, Leisure, Community and Everyday Life*. New York: Basic Books.

———. 2013. "More Losers Than Winners in America's New Economic Geography." *Bloomberg City Lab*, January 30. https://www.bloomberg.com/news/articles/2013-01-30/more-losers-than-winners-in-america-s-new-economic-geography.

———. 2017. *The New Urban Crisis: How Cities Are Increasing Inequality, Deepening Segregation, and Failing the Middle Class—And What We Can Do About It*. New York: Basic Books.

Folkets Hus och Parker. 2020. "The National Federation of People's Parks and Community Centres" (In Swedish). https://www.folketshusochparker.se/medlemmar/.

Franzén, Mats. 2005. "New Social Movements and Gentrification in Hamburg and Stockholm: A Comparative Study." *Journal of Housing and the Built Environment* 20 (1): 51–77. https://doi.org/10.1007/s10901-005-6764-z.

Franzén, Mats, Nils Hertting, and Catharina Thörn. 2016. *Stad till Salu: Entreprenörsurbanismen och Det Offentliga Rummets Värde*. Göteborg: Daidalos.

Gamson, Joshua. 1997. "Messages of Exclusion: Gender, Movements, and Symbolic Boundaries." *Gender and Society* 11 (2): 178–199. https://doi.org/10.1177/089124397011002003.

Gerbaudo, Paolo. 2012. *Tweets and the Streets: Social Media and Contemporary Activism*. London: Pluto Press.

———. 2014. "Spikey Posters: Street Media and Territoriality in Urban Activist Scenes." *Space and Culture* 17 (3): 239–250.

Gibril, Suzan. 2018. "Shifting Spaces of Contention: An Analysis of the Ultras' Mobilization in Revolutionary Egypt." *European Journal of Turkish Studies: Social Sciences on Contemporary Turkey* 26. https://doi.org/10.4000/ejts.5835.

Giddens, Anthony. 1984. *The Constitution of Society: Outline of the Theory of Structuration*. Berkeley: University of California Press.

Gilbert, Liette, and Mustafa Dikeç. 2008. "Right to the City: The Politics of Citizenship." In *Space, Difference, Everyday Life: Reading Henri Lefebvre*, edited by Kanishka Goonewardena, Stefan Kipfer, Richard Milgrom and Christian Schmid, 250–261. New York: Routledge.

Glass, Pepper. 2010. "Everyday Routines in Free Spaces: Explaining the Persistence of The Zapatistas in Los Angeles." *Mobilization* 15 (2): 199–216. https://doi.org/10.17813/maiq.15.2.ah34865736071251.

Gordon, Uri. 2018. "Prefigurative Politics between Ethical Practice and Absent Promise." *Political Studies* 66 (2): 521–537. https://doi.org/10.1177/00323217 17722363.

Gould, Deborah. 2001. "Rock the Boat, Don't Rock the Boat, Baby: Ambivalence and the Emergence of Militant AIDS Activism." In *Passionate Politics: Emotions and Social Movements*, edited by Jeff Goodwin, James M. Jasper, and Francesca Polletta, 135–157. Chicago: University of Chicago Press.

Goyens, Tom. 2009. *Beer and Revolution: The German Anarchist Movement in New York City, 1880–1914*. Urbana: University of Illinois Press.

Grahn-Hinnfors, Gunilla, and Linus Hugo 2009. "Våg av Husockupationer." *Göteborgs-Posten*, September 27. http://www.gp.se/nyheter/goteborg/1.212635-vag-av-husockupationer.

Granström, Kjell. 2002. "Göteborgskravallerna." Report 187. Styrelsen för Psykologiskt Försvar. https://rib.msb.se/filer/pdf/22857.pdf.

Grassman, Eva Jeppsson, and Lars Svedberg. 2006. "Civic Participation in the Welfare State: Patterns in Contemporary Sweden." In *State and Civil Society in Northern Europe: The Swedish Model Reconsidered*, edited by Lars Trägårdh, 126–164. New York: Berghahn Books.

Greenberg, Miriam, and Penny Lewis. 2017. *The City Is the Factory: New Solidarities and Spatial Strategies in an Urban Age*. Ithaca, NY: Cornell University Press.

Gundelach, Peter. 1990. "New Social Movements in the Nordic Countries." In *Scandinavia in a New Europe*, edited by Thomas P. Boje, 330–348. Oslo: Scandinavian University Press.

Hajighasemi, Ali. 2004. *The Transformation of the Swedish Welfare System: Fact or Fiction?: Globalisation, Institutions and Welfare State Change in a Social Democratic Regime*. Huddinge, Sweden: Södertörns högskola.

Hall, Stuart, and Tony Jefferson. 1975. *Resistance through Rituals: Youth Subcultures in Post-War Britain*. London: Routledge.

Hallstan, Leif. 1983. "Nya Anarkismen Samlar Sig . . ." *Arbetaren*, December 2, p. 3.

Halvorsen, Sam. 2017. "Spatial Dialectics and the Geography of Social Movements: The Case of Occupy London." *Transactions of the Institute of British Geographers* 42 (3): 445–457.

Hansen, Christina. 2019. "Solidarity in Diversity: Activism as a Pathway of Migrant Emplacement in Malmö," Ph.D. diss., Malmö University. https://doi.org/10.24834/isbn.9789178770175.

———. 2020. "Alliances, Friendships, and Alternative Structures: Solidarity among Radical Left Activists and Precarious Migrants in Malmö." *Jour-*

nal of Race, Ethnicity and the City 1: 1–2, 67–86. https://doi.org/10.1080
/26884674.2020.1797600.

Harvey, David. 2003. "The Right to the City." *International Journal of Urban and Regional Research* 27 (4): 939–941.

———. 2012. *Rebel Cities: From the Right to the City to the Urban Revolution.* London: Verso Books.

Haunss, Sebastian, and Darcy K. Leach. 2007. "Social Movement Scenes: Infrastructures of Opposition in Civil Society." In *Civil Societies and Social Movements: Potentials and Problems*, edited by Derrick Purdue, 71–99. London: Routledge.

Hebdige, Dick. 1979. *Subculture: The Meaning of Style.* London: Methuen.

Hedin, Karin, Eric Clark, Emma Lundholm, and Gunnar Malmberg. 2012. "Neoliberalization of Housing in Sweden: Gentrification, Filtering, and Social Polarization." *Annals of the Association of American Geographers* 102 (2): 443–463. https://doi.org/10.1080/00045608.2011.620508.

Hedlund, Johanna, and Axel Gagge. 2009. "Kampen om Staden Har Bara Börjat." *Direkt Aktion* 57: 6–9.

Hesmondhalgh, David. 2005. "Subcultures, Scenes or Tribes? None of the Above." *Journal of Youth Studies* 8 (1): 21–40. https://doi.org/10.1080/1367 6260500063652.

Hodkinson, Stuart, and Paul Chatterton. 2006. "Autonomy in the City? Reflections on the Social Centres Movement in the UK." *City* 10 (3): 305–315. https://doi.org/10.1080/13604810600982222.

Holm, Andrej, and Armin Kuhn. 2017. "Squatting and Urban Renewal: The Interaction of Squatter Movements and Strategies of Urban Restructuring in Berlin." *International Journal of Urban and Regional Research* 35 (3): 644–658. https://doi.org/10.1111/j.1468-2427.2010.001009.x.

Holmberg, Ingrid. 2002. "'Where the Past Is Still Alive': Variation over the Identity of Haga, in Göteborg." In *The Construction of Built Heritage: A North European Perspective on Policies, Practices, and Outcomes*, edited by Angela Phelps, G. J. Ashworth, and Bengt O. H. Johansson, 59–73. Aldershot, UK: Ashgate.

Höök, Lovisa. 2012. "Möllans Väg Mot City." *Sydsvenskan*, January 24. http://www.sydsvenskan.se/malmo/mollans-vag-mot-city/.

Hospers, Gert-Jan. 2006. "Borders, Bridges and Branding: The Transformation of the Øresund Region into an Imagined Space." *European Planning Studies* 14 (8): 1015–1033. https://doi.org/10.1080/09654310600852340.

Hospers, Gert-Jan, and Cees-Jan Pen. 2008. "A View on Creative Cities beyond the Hype." *Creativity and Innovation Management* 17 (4): 259–270. https://doi.org/10.1111/j.1467-8691.2008.00498.x.

Ingman, Gustav. 2009. "Att Investera i Nedskärningar." *Direkt Aktion* (60–61): 20–21.

Irwin, John. 1973. "Surfing: The Natural History of an Urban Scene." *Urban Life and Culture* 2 (2): 131–160. https://doi.org/10.1177/089124167300200201.

———. 1977. *Scenes.* Beverly Hills, CA: SAGE.

Jacobsson, Kerstin, and Adrienne Sörbom. 2015. "After a Cycle of Contention: Post-Gothenburg Strategies of Left-Libertarian Activists in Sweden." *Social Movement Studies* 14 (6): 713–732.

Jämte, Jan. 2013. "Antirasismens Många Ansikten." Ph.D. diss., Umeå universitet. https://www.diva-portal.org/smash/record.jsf?pid=diva2%3A1413058&dswid=3009.

Jämte, Jan, Måns Lundstedt, and Magnus Wennerhag. 2020. "From Radical Counterculture to Pragmatic Radicalism? The Collective Identity of Contemporary Radical Left-Libertarian Activism in Sweden." *Journal for the Study of Radicalism* 14 (1): 1–36. https://doi.org/10.14321/jstudradi.14.1.0001.

Jämte, Jan, and Adrienne Sörbom. 2016. "Why Did It Not Happen Here? The Gradual Radicalization of the Anarchist Movement in Sweden 1980–90." In *A European Youth Revolt,* edited by Knud Andresen and Bart van der Steen, 97–111. London: Palgrave Macmillan.

Kahn, Richard, and Douglas Kellner. 2004. "New Media and Internet Activism: From the 'Battle of Seattle' to Blogging." *New Media Society* 6 (1): 87–95. https://doi.org/10.1177/1461444804039908.

Kapsylen. 2020. http://www.kapsylen.se/index.html.

Karlsson, Lennart. 2009. "Arbetarrörelsen, Folkets Hus och Offentligheten i Bromölla 1905–1960." Ph.D. diss., Växjö University. https://www.diva-portal.org/smash/record.jsf?pid=diva2%3A206398&dswid=821.

Kärrholm, Mattias, and Johan Wirdelöv. 2019. "The Neighbourhood in Pieces: The Fragmentation of Local Public Space in a Swedish Housing Area." *International Journal of Urban and Regional Research* 43 (5): 870–887. https://doi.org/10.1111/1468-2427.12735.

Katsiaficas, George N. 2006. *The Subversion of Politics: European Autonomous Social Movements and the Decolonization of Everyday Life.* Oakland, CA: AK Press.

King, Lester O., and Jeffrey S. Lowe. 2018. "'We Want to Do It Differently': Resisting Gentrification in Houston's Northern Third Ward." *Journal of Urban Affairs* 40 (8): 1161–1176. https://doi.org/10.1080/07352166.2018.1495039.

Kontrapunkt Collective. 2012. "Om Kontrapunkt." Pamphlet.

———. 2020. "Kontrapunkt: Vi Ger Upp Drömmen om Malmös Solidariska Hjärta." *Brand* 2 (February 24). https://tidningenbrand.se/2020/02/24/kontrapunkt-vi-ger-upp-drommen-om-malmos-solidariska-hjarta/.

Landsorganisationen i Sverige. 2007. "The Swedish Trade Union Confederation-Facts and History." http://www.lo.se/home/lo/home.nsf/unidview/A3E9A303B74321E5C12572E300410A32/$file/LO%20Swedish%20Trade%20Union%20Confederation%20ENG.pdf.

Larsson, Arne. 2001. "Därför slog polisen till." *Göteborgs-Posten*, June 15, p. 35.

Larsson, Jimmie. 2017. "Kontrapunkt Tvingas Lägga Ner Sitt Sociala Arbete." Sveriges Radio P4. https://sverigesradio.se/artikel/6697022.

Lauermann, John. 2018. "Geographies of Mega-Urbanization." *Geography Compass* 12 (8): e12396.

Leach, Darcy, and Sebastian Haunss. 2009. "Social Movement Scenes." In *Culture, Social Movements, and Protest*, edited by Hank Johnston, 255–276. Burlington, VT: Ashgate.

Lefebvre, Henri. (1968) 1996. "Right to the City." In *Writings on Cities*, edited by Eleonore Kofman and Elizabeth Lebas, 63–184. Oxford, UK: Blackwell.

Leslie, Deborah. 2005. "Creative Cities?" *Geoforum* 36 (4): 403–405. https://doi.org/10.1016/j.geoforum.2005.02.001.

Levy, Diane K, Jennifer Comey, and Sandra Padilla. 2006. "In the Face of Gentrification: Case Studies of Local Efforts to Mitigate Displacement." *Urban Institute* 16 (3): 238–315.

Lindvall, Johannes, and Bo Rothstein. 2006. "Sweden: The Fall of the Strong State." *Scandinavian Political Studies* 29 (1): 47–63. https://doi.org/10.1111/j.1467-9477.2006.00141.x.

Lloyd, Richard. 2006. *Neo-Bohemia: Art and Commerce in the Postindustrial City*. New York: Routledge.

Malmö City Library. Newspaper Clippings, Möllevången Neighborhood Collection, Malmö, Sweden.

Malmö Stad. 2000. "Områdesfakta—Möllevången-00." http://www.malmo.se/download/18.d2883b1055ac55112800041/1383648072749/036.+M%C3%B6llev%C3%A5ngen.pdf.

———. 2008. "Områdesfakta—Möllevången-08." http://www.malmo.se/download/18.41e3f87712038946594800343/1383648123856/038.M%C3%B6llev%C3%A5ngen.pdf (accessed 8 October 2013).

———. 2014. "Vad Hander i Malmö?" http://www.malmo.se/Turist.html.

———. 2019. "Statistik för Malmös Områden 2019." https://malmo.se/Fakta-och-statistik/Statistik-for-Malmos-omraden.html.

Malmö Stadskontoret. 2012. "Malmöläget: Statistik och Fakta om Näringslivet i Malmö." http://www.malmobusiness.com/sites/default/files/filearchive/malmolaget_2012.pdf.

Marschan-Piekkari, Rebecca, and Cristina Reis. 2004. "Language and Languages in Cross-Cultural Interviewing." In *Handbook of Qualitative Research Methods for International Business*, edited by Rebecca Piekkari and Catherine Welch, 224–243. New York: Elgar.

Martin, Greg. 2015. *Understanding Social Movements*. London: Routledge.

Martínez, Miguel. 2020. *Squatters in the Capitalist City: Housing, Justice, and Urban Politics*. London: Routledge.

Martínez López, Miguel A. 2018. *The Urban Politics of Squatters' Movements*. Palgrave Macmillan.

Maxwell, Joseph. 2013. *Qualitative Research Design: An Interactive Approach.* Thousand Oaks, CA: SAGE.

Mayer, Margit. 2016. "Neoliberal Urbanism and Uprisings Across Europe." In *Urban Uprisings: Challenging Neoliberal Urbanism in Europe*, edited by Margit Mayer, Catharina Thörn, and Håkan Thörn, 57–92. London: Palgrave Macmillan UK. https://doi.org/10.1057/978-1-137-50509-5_2.

McFarlane, Colin. 2009. "Translocal Assemblages: Space, Power and Social Movements." *Geoforum* 40 (4): 561–567.

Melucci, Alberto. 1989. *Nomads of the Present: Social Movements and Individual Needs in Contemporary Society.* New York: Hutchinson Radius.

———. 1996. *Challenging Codes: Collective Action in the Information Age.* New York: Cambridge University Press.

Micheletti, Michele. 1995. *Civil Society and State Relations in Sweden.* Brookfield, VT: Ashgate.

Mische, Ann. 2009. "Projects and Possibilities: Researching Futures in Action." *Sociological Forum* 24 (3): 694–704. https://doi.org/10.1111/j.1573-7861.2009.01127.x.

———. 2014. "Measuring Futures in Action: Projective Grammars in the Rio +20 Debates." *Theory and Society* 43 (3–4): 437–464.

Möllevångsfestivalen. 2010. "Om Festivalen." http://mollevangsfestivalen.wordpress.com/about/.

Möllevångsgruppen. 2010a. "Historik." http://mollevangsgruppen.wordpress.com/om-gruppen/historik/.

———. 2010b. "Vad Gör Vi?" http://mollevangsgruppen.wordpress.com/vad-gor-vi/.

Mudu, Pierpaolo. 2004. "Resisting and Challenging Neoliberalism: The Development of Italian Social Centers." *Antipode* 36 (5): 917–941. https://doi.org/10.1111/j.1467-8330.2004.00461.x.

Muggleton, David. 2005. "From Classlessness to Clubculture: A Genealogy of Post-War British Youth Cultural Analysis." *Young* 13 (2): 205. https://doi.org/10.1177/1103308805051322.

Muggleton, David, and Rupert Weinzierl. 2003. *The Post-Subcultures Reader.* New York: Berg.

Naegler, Laura. 2012. *Gentrification and Resistance: Cultural Criminology, Control, and the Commodification of Urban Protest in Hamburg.* Münster, Germany: LIT Verlag.

Nandorf, Tove. 2001. "Över 200 Greps efter Kravaller." *Dagens Nyheter*, June 15, p. A6.

Newman, Kathe, and Elvin K. Wyly. 2006. "The Right to Stay Put, Revisited: Gentrification and Resistance to Displacement in New York City." *Urban Studies* 43 (1): 23–57. https://doi.org/10.1080/004209805003887.

Nicholls, Walter. 2009. "Place, Networks, Space: Theorising the Geographies of Social Movements." *Transactions of the Institute of British Geographers* 34 (1): 78–93. https://doi.org/10.1111/j.1475-5661.2009.00331.x.

Nicholls, Walter, Byron Miller, and Justin Beaumont. 2013. *Spaces of Contention: Spatialities and Social Movements.* Farnham, UK: Ashgate.

Nwachukwu, Mathilda. 2010. "Än Finns det Hopp för Kulturhuset Underjorden." *Göteborgs Fria*, October 26. http://www.goteborgsfria.se/artikel /85754.

Olsen, Gregg M. 2002. *The Politics of the Welfare State: Canada, Sweden and the United States.* New York: Oxford University Press.

Olsson, Petra. 2010a. "Möllevångsfestivalen Vill Ha ett Möllan åt Alla." *Skånes Fria*, June 24. http://www.skanesfria.se/artikel/84376.

———. 2010b. "Stad Solidar Vill Bygga Bort Gentrifieringen på Möllan." *Skånes Fria*, October 20. http://www.skanesfria.se/artikel/85686.

Palmkvist, Joakim. 2009. "'De Ville Slå mot Utkanten som Helhet.'" *Sydsvenskan*, November 30. http://www.sydsvenskan.se/malmo/de-ville-sla-mot -utkanten-som-helhet/.

Paulsen, Krista E. 2004. "Making Character Concrete: Empirical Strategies for Studying Place Distinction." *City and Community* 3 (3): 243–262. https://doi .org/10.1111/j.1535-6841.2004.00080.x.

Pearsall, Hamil. 2013. "Superfund Me: A Study of Resistance to Gentrification in New York City." *Urban Studies* 50 (11): 2293–2310. https://doi.org/10.1177 /0042098013478236.

Pecile, Veronica. 2017. "Urban Mobilisations in a Post-Crisis Mediterranean City: The Case of Commons in Palermo." *Comparative Law Review* 8 (1): 1–16.

Peck, Jamie. 2005. "Struggling with the Creative Class." *International Journal of Urban and Regional Research* 29 (4): 740–770. https://doi.org/10.1111/j.1468 -2427.2005.00620.x.

Pell, Susan. 2014. "Mobilizing Urban Publics, Imagining Democratic Possibilities: Reading the Politics of Urban Redevelopment in Discourses of Gentrification and Revitalization." *Cultural Studies* 28 (1): 29–48.

Pérez, Gina. 2004. *The Near Northwest Side Story: Migration, Displacement, and Puerto Rican Families.* Berkeley: University of California Press.

Peterson, Abby, Håkan Thörn, and Mattias Wahlström. 2018. "Sweden 1950– 2015: Contentious Politics and Social Movements between Confrontation and Conditioned Cooperation." In *Popular Struggle and Democracy in Scandinavia: 1700–Present*, edited by Flemming Mikkelsen, Knut Kjeldstadli, and Stefan Nyzell, 377–432. London: Palgrave Macmillan UK.

Pierce, Joseph, Deborah Martin, and James Murphy. 2010. "Relational Place-Making: The Networked Politics of Place." *Transactions of the Institute of British Geographers* 36 (1): 54–70. https://doi.org/10.1111/j.1475-5661.2010 .00411.x.

Piotrowski, Grzegorz, and Magnus Wennerhag. 2015. "Always against the State? An Analysis of Polish and Swedish Radical Left-Libertarian Activists' Interaction with Institutionalized Politics." *Partecipazione e conflitto* 8 (3): 845–875.

Polanska, Dominika V. 2019. *Contentious Politics and the Welfare State: Squatting in Sweden*. London: Routledge.

Polletta, Francesca. 1999. "'Free Spaces' in Collective Action." *Theory and Society* 28 (1): 1–38. https://doi.org/10.1002/9780470674871.wbespm094.

Popenoe, David. 2001. *Private Pleasure, Public Plight: Urban Development, Suburban Sprawl, and the Decline of Community*. Piscataway, NJ: Transaction.

Pred, Allan. 1984. "Place as Historically Contingent Process: Structuration and Time-Geography of Becoming Places." *Annals of the Association of American Geographers* 74 (2): 279–297. https://doi.org/10.1111/j.1467-8306.1984.tb01453.x.

———. 2000. *Even in Sweden: Racisms, Racialized Spaces and the Popular Geographical Imagination*. Berkeley: University of California Press.

Pries, Johan, Erik Jönsson, and Don Mitchell. 2020. "Parks and Houses for the People." *Places: The Journal of Public Scholarship on Architecture, Landscape, and Urbanism*. https://placesjournal.org/article/swedish-social-democratic-parks-and-houses-for-the-people/.

Pries, Johan, and Karin Zackari. 2016. "'Här Slutar Sverige': Ockupationen på Ringgatan i Malmö 1990." In *Politik Underifrån: Kollektiva Konfrontationer under Sveriges 1900-Tal*, edited by Andrés Brink Pinto and Martin Ericsson, 193–210. Lund, Sweden: Arkiv.

Pruijt, Hans. 2003. "Is the Institutionalization of Urban Movements Inevitable? A Comparison of the Opportunities for Sustained Squatting in New York City and Amsterdam." *International Journal of Urban and Regional Research* 27 (1): 133–157. https://doi.org/10.1111/1468-2427.00436.

———. 2013. "The Logic of Urban Squatting." *International Journal of Urban and Regional Research* 37 (1): 19–45. https://doi.org/10.1111/j.1468-2427.2012.01116.x.

Purcell, Mark. 2002. "Excavating Lefebvre: The Right to the City and Its Urban Politics of the Inhabitant." *GeoJournal* 58: 99–108. https://doi.org/10.1023/B:GEJO.0000010829.62237.8f.

———. 2008. *Recapturing Democracy: Neoliberalization and the Struggle for Alternative Urban Futures*. New York: Routledge.

Pusey, Andre. 2010. "Social Centres and the New Cooperativism of the Common." *Affinities: A Journal of Radical Theory, Culture, and Action*. http://eprints.leedsbeckett.ac.uk/id/eprint/2426/.

Rabbat, Nasser. 2012. "The Arab Revolution Takes Back the Public Space." *Critical Inquiry* 39 (1): 198–208. https://doi.org/10.1086/668055.

Radio Sweden. 2012. "Independent Artists Rebuild Their Dream." September 13. http://sverigesradio.se/sida/artikel.aspx?programid=2054&artikel=5269593.

RåFilm. 2002. *Möllevången—Adjö?* http://vimeo.com/43992290.

Rayman, Sanna, and Per Gudmundson. 2008. "Hjälp Till att Bygga Upp Cyklopen Ugen." *Svenska Dagbladet*, February 7. http://www.svd.se/opinion/ledarsidan/hjalp-till-att-bygga-upp-cyklopen-igen_2158245.svd.

Ruggiero, Vincenzo. 2001. *Movements in the City: Conflict in the European Metropolis*. Upper Saddle River, NJ: Prentice Hall.

Säkerhetspolisen. 2009. "Våldsam Politisk Extremism: Antidemokratiska Grupperingar på Yttersta Höger- Och Vänsterkanten." Report by the Swedish Security Service. http://www.sakerhetspolisen.se/download/18.635d 23c2141933256ea1fcb/1381154798654/valdsampolitiskextremism.pdf.

Sandén, Salka. 2007. *Deltagänget*. Stockholm: Vertigo.

Sassen, Saskia. 2011. "The Global Street: Making the Political." *Globalizations* 8 (5): 573–579. https://doi.org/10.1080/14747731.2011.622458.

Schütz, Alfred. 1951. "Choosing Among Projects of Action." *Philosophy and Phenomenological Research* 12:161–84.

Sernhede, Ove, Catharina Thörn, and Håkan Thörn. 2016. "The Stockholm Uprising in Context: Urban Social Movements in the Rise and Demise of the Swedish Welfare-State City." In *Urban Uprisings: Challenging Neoliberal Urbanism in Europe*, edited by Margit Mayer, Catharina Thörn, and Håkan Thörn, 149–173. London: Palgrave Macmillan UK. https://doi.org/10.1057 /978-1-137-50509-5_5.

Shiffman, Ronald, Rick Bell, Lance Jay Brown, and Lynne Elizabeth, eds. 2012. *Beyond Zuccotti Park: Freedom of Assembly and the Occupation of Public Space*. Oakland, CA: New Village Press.

Simi, Pete, and Robert Futrell. 2010. *American Swastika: Inside the White Power Movement's Hidden Spaces of Hate*. Lanham, MD: Rowman and Littlefield.

Slater, Tom. 2006. "The Eviction of Critical Perspectives from Gentrification Research." *International Journal of Urban and Regional Research* 30 (4): 737–757.

Sörbom, Adrienne. 2005. *När Vardagen Blir Politik*. Stockholm: Atlas.

Spain, Daphne. 2016. *Constructive Feminism: Women's Spaces and Women's Rights in the American City*. Ithaca, NY: Cornell University Press.

Stad Solidar. 2010. "Stad Solidar Manifesto." Pamphlet.

Staggenborg, Suzanne. 1998. "Social Movement Communities and Cycles of Protest: The Emergence and Maintenance of a Local Women's Movement." *Social Problems* 45 (2): 180–204. https://doi.org/10.2307/3097243.

———. 2013. "Organization and Community in Social Movements." In *The Future of Social Movement Research: Dynamics, Mechanisms and Processes*, edited by Jacquelien van Stekelenburg, Conny Roggeband, and Bert Klandermans, 125–144. Minneapolis: University of Minnesota Press.

Stahl, Geoff. 2004. "'It's Like Canada Reduced': Setting the Scene in Montreal." In *After Subculture: Critical Studies in Contemporary Youth Culture*, edited by Andy Bennett and Keith Kahn-Harris, 51–64. New York: Palgrave Macmillan.

Ståhl, Margareta. 2005. *Möten och Människor: I Folkets Hus och Folkets Park*. Stockholm: Atlas.

Stahre, Ulf. 1999. *Den Alternativa Staden: Stockholms Stadsomvandling och By-alagsrorelsen*. Stockholm: Stockholmia Förlag.

Statens Offentliga Utredningar. 2002. "Hotet Från Vänster: Säkerhetstjänsternas Övervakning av Kommunister, Anarkister m.m. 1965–2002." http:// www.regeringen.se/sb/d/108/a/450.

Stockholms Stad. 2020. "Om Stockholms Stad." https://start.stockholm/om -stockholms-stad/.

Straw, Will. 2004. "Cultural Scenes." *Society and Leisure* 27 (2): 411–422. https:// doi.org/10.1080/07053436.2004.10707657.

Swain, Daniel. 2019. "Not Not but Not Yet: Present and Future in Prefigurative Politics." *Political Studies* 67 (1): 47–62. https://doi.org/10.1177/003232 1717741233.

Ta Tillbaka Välfärden. 2010a. "Öppna Upp Stockholm!—Gatufest 8:E Maj." http://ockupantscenen.se/stockholm/75.

———. 2010b. "Ta Tillbaka Välfärden—Dags för en Ny Utopikarneval!" http://motkraft.net/2011/03/11/ta-tillbaka-valfarden-den-internationella -revolutionen-sprider-sig-dags-for-en-ny-utopikarneval/.

Taylor, Verta. 1989. "Social Movement Continuity: The Women's Movement in Abeyance." *American Sociological Review* 54 (5): 761–775. https://doi.org/10 .2307/2117752.

Thörn, Catharina. 2011. "Soft Policies of Exclusion: Entrepreneurial Strategies of Ambiance and Control of Public Space in Gothenburg, Sweden." *Urban Geography* 32 (7): 989–1008. https://doi.org/10.2747/0272-3638.32.7.989.

Thörn, Catharina, and Håkan Thörn. 2017. "Swedish Cities Now Belong to the Most Segregated in Europe." *Sociologisk Forskning* 54 (4): 293–296.

Thörn, Håkan. 1999. "Nya Sociala Rörelser och Politikens Globalisering: Demokrati utanför Parlamentet?" In *Civilsamhället*, edited by E. Amnå, 425–468. Stockholm: Demokratiutredningen.

———. 2012a. "Governing Movements in Urban Space." In *Transformations of the Swedish Welfare State*, edited by B. Larsson, Martin Letell, and Håkan Thörn, 199–214. New York: Palgrave Macmillan.

———. 2012b. "In between Social Engineering and Gentrification: Urban Restructuring, Social Movements, and the Place Politics of Open Space." *Journal of Urban Affairs* 34 (2): 153–168. https://doi.org/10.1111/j.1467-9906.2012 .00608.x.

———. 2013. *Stad i Rörelse: Stadsomvandlingen och Striderna om Haga och Christiania*. Stockholm: Bokförlaget Atlas.

Trägårdh, Lars. 2006. *State and Civil Society in Northern Europe: The Swedish Model Reconsidered*. New York: Berghahn Books.

Tsang, Eric W. K. 1998. "Inside Story: Mind Your Identity When Conducting Cross-National Research." *Organization Studies* 19 (3): 511–515. https://doi .org/10.1177/017084069801900307.

"Utkanten Guide." 2010. Pamphlet.

Vandenberg, Andrew. 2006. "Social-Movement Unionism in Theory and in Sweden." *Social Movement Studies* 5 (2): 171–191. https://doi.org/10.1080 /14742830600807584.

van Stekelenburg, Jacquelien, and Conny Roggeband. 2013. "Introduction: The Future of Social Movement Research." In *The Future of Social Movement Research: Dynamics, Mechanisms and Processes*, edited by Jacquelien van Stekelenburg, Conny Roggeband, and Bert Klandermans, 11–21. Minneapolis: University of Minnesota Press.

Vasudevan, Alex. 2017. *The Autonomous City: A History of Urban Squatting*. New York: Verso Books.

Visit Sweden. 2013. "Södermalm." http://www.visitstockholm.com/en/To-Do /Tips/Shopping-Sodermalm/.

Wåg, Mattias. 2010. "Först Tar Vi ett Hus . . . Sedan Hela Staden." *Brand* 1: 26–27.

Wagner-Pacifici, Robin, and Colin E. Ruggero. 2018. "Temporal Blindspots in Occupy Philadelphia." *Social Movement Studies*. https://doi.org/10.1080 /14742837.2018.1474096.

Wang, Stephen Wei-Hsin. 2011. "Commercial Gentrification and Entrepreneurial Governance in Shanghai: A Case Study of Taikang Road Creative Cluster." *Urban Policy and Research* 29 (4): 363–380. https://doi.org/10.1080 /08111146.2011.598226.

Watt, Paul. 2009. "Housing Stock Transfers, Regeneration and State-Led Gentrification in London." *Urban Policy and Research* 27 (3): 229–242. https:// doi.org/10.1080/08111140903154147.

Wennerhag, Magnus, Hilma Holm, Johan Lindgren, Henrik Nordvall, and Adrienne Sörbom. 2006. "Göteborgskravallerna Skadade Demonstranters Demokratisyn." *Dagens Nyheter*, June 15. http://www.dn.se/debatt/gote borgskravallerna-skadade-demonstranters-demokratisyn.

Whittier, Nancy. 1995. *Feminist Generations: The Persistence of the Radical Women's Movement*. Philadelphia: Temple University Press.

Yates, Luke. 2014. "Rethinking Prefiguration: Alternatives, Micropolitics and Goals in Social Movements." *Social Movement Studies* 13 (1): 1–21. https:// doi.org/10.1080/14742837.2013.870883.

———. 2020. "Prefigurative Politics and Social Movement Strategy: The Roles of Prefiguration in the Reproduction, Mobilisation and Coordination of Movements." *Political Studies*, July 2020. https://doi.org/10.1177 /0032321720936046.

Yip, Ngai-ming, Miguel Angel Martínez López, and Xiaoyi Sun, eds. 2019. *Contested Cities and Urban Activism*. Singapore: Palgrave Macmillan. https:// doi.org/10.1007/978-981-13-1730-9.

Zackariasson, Maria. 2006. *Viljan att Förändra Världen: Politisk Engagemang Hos Unga i den Globala Rättviserörelsen*. Umeå, Sweden: Boréa.

Zukin, Sharon. 2009. "Changing Landscapes of Power: Opulence and the Urge for Authenticity." *International Journal of Urban and Regional Research* 33 (2): 543–553. https://doi.org/10.1111/j.1468-2427.2009.00867.x.

———. 2010. *Naked City: The Death and Life of Authentic Urban Places.* New York: Oxford University Press.

Zukin, Sharon, Valerie Trujillo, Peter Frase, Danielle Jackson, Tim Recuber, and Abraham Walker. 2009. "New Retail Capital and Neighborhood Change: Boutiques and Gentrification in New York City." *City and Community* 8 (1): 47–64. https://doi.org/10.1111/j.1540-6040.2009.01269.x.

Index

abeyance structures, 10–11
Alarm Stockholm 113, 116–117
anarchism, 15, 32, 35–37, 60, 68, 102, 133, 142
anarchist Book Fair (Stockholm), 142–143, 153
anarcho-syndicalism. *See* Syndicalism
anti-capitalism, 3–4, 12, 17, 22, 35, 43, 46, 60, 64, 68, 69, 78, 86
antifascism, 37, 133–134
appropriation of public space, (see Right to the City)
assemblages, 15
autonomous social movements. Characteristics and definition of, 4; conflict in, 71–72; Denmark, 35–36, 42; France, 16; Germany, 13, 17, 35–36; Italy, 17; Netherlands, 35; Spain, 62

brand (anarchist magazine), 32, 34, 42, 104, 136, 141, 143, 158
building codes, 57, 61, 70–71

Café Hängmattan, 109
civil society, 29–30

creative city policies, 84–86, 113
collective effervescence, 140–141
consensus, 29, 61, 135
contingency, 154
counterculture, 4, 8, 62–63, 103, 113, 120–121, 134
cultural havens, 9
Cyklopen (Stockholm), see Social Centers

Dagens Nyheter (newspaper), 54, 121, 158
diffusion of ideas, 47–48, 92–95
disillusionment, 37, 44
do-it-yourself (DIY), 37, 49, 54, 59, 61, 71, 128–129, 139, 161

ethnicity, 22, 50–51, 85
exchange value, 12
exclusion, 134, 143–146, 150

gender, 24, 50, 70–72, 76, 99
gentrification, 1, 4, 5–7,13–14, 17, 24, 82–89, 91, 96, 99, 116–117, 120–124; autonomous movement responses to,

180 \ Index

gentrification (*continued*)
4, 14, 24, 89–96, 110, 152; commercial, 13, 88, 91, 95, 116; displacement, 4, 152; ethnicity and, 22; slowing the process of, 7, 13; social class and, 19, 22, 96–97, 99; squatting and, 41; welfare state and, 5–7
Glassfabriken café, 2–3
Göteborg. Battle over Göteborg campaign, 122–123

history 21–22, 113, 118–121; Haga neighborhood, 113, 118–121; reputation as radical, 40; riots in 2001, 37–41, 51; suburbs, 121–124
historic preservation, 28, 43, 120–121, 123
Högdalen, 53, 55, 76, 109, 117, 126
housing, 5–7, 18–19, 41–42, 85, 96–97

illegal activity, 17, 40, 57, 65, 138

Kafé 44 (Stockholm). *See also* social centers
Kontrapunkt (Malmö). *See* social centers
Kulturhuset Underjorden (Göteborg). *See* social centers

labor movement (in Sweden), 19, 31–34, 48–49, 58–59, 81–82, 113–114

Malmö. City tunnel, 87; connection to Copenhagen, 84–85; history, 19–20; Möllevången neighborhood, 2, 4, 50, 56, 83–108; Möllevångsfestivalen (street festival), 4–5, 89–96, 153; Möllevångsgruppen (neighborhood association), 83–89, 105–106; Rosengård neighborhood, 50–51; Stad Solidar project, 96–100
media (grassroots), 63–66, 133. *See also* brand
methodology, 23–25, 157–161; comparative case analysis, 5, 23–24, 157; ethnography, 23–24, 157; gaining

access, 159–161; interviews, 158–159; language, 157–158
Million Program (miljonprogrammet), 6

neighborhood movement (byalagsrörelsen), 6, 35, 41, 88, 113–116
new social movements, 34–35, 114, 116

occupation. *See* squatting
old left. *See* labor movement
Öresund region, 21, 84–85, 87–88

people's houses, 58–60, 153
people's kitchens, 52, 66
people's movements, 31
People's Park, 81, 82, 86, 89, 90, 105
pirate cinema (piratbio), 63–66
prefigurative politics, 47–48, 61–78, 69–70, 148; definition of, 47; projectivity and 11, 70, 73

relationships, 140–146
retreat structures, 43, 151
right to the city, 7, 11–12, 42, 91–93, 101, 106–107, 117, 122–124, 151–153, 156

safe spaces, 9
social centers. activities in, 61, 65, 103–104; arson at, 55, 73, 75, 79, 126, 144, 154; Cyklopen (Stockholm), 53, 69–78, 126–127, 135; Kafé 44 (Stockholm), 132–135; Kontrapunkt (Malmö), 3, 51, 100–104; Kulturhuset Underjorden (Göteborg) 50, 52–53, 66, 79, 119, 121–122, 124, 128, 131, 144–146, 151; norms, 66–69; self-management and, 59–60; Ungdomshuset (Copenhagen), 42; Utkanten (Malmö), 50, 55–57, 151
social democracy, 2, 5–7, 32–33, 44–46, 59, 71, 81
social movement community, 10
social movement scenes. characteristics and definition of, 4, 7–11, 15–17,

149–150; Europe, 14; experimentation in, 47, 61–63, 68, 103, 150; fledgling scene (Göteborg), 11, 110, 127–132, 143–146; fragile scene (Stockholm), 110, 139–143; free spaces and, 9; functional view of, 4, 9–10, 150; outcomes of, 111, 139–147, 149; social centers and, 49–52, 58; social movement culture and, 8–11; spatial dimensions of, 3–4, 8, 14–16, 98, 110–112, 118, 124–125, 132, 146–147, 149, 52; strong scene (Malmö), 83, 108, 110, 139

squatting, 13, 16, 41–44, 45, 48, 62, 70, 89, 94, 109–110, 116–118, 120, 128, 136, 141, 147, 154, 158; conservational squatting, 42–43; entrepreneurial squatting, 42–44; Husnallarna (squatters in the 1980), 121; limitations of, 99, 136–138, 147, 154; political squatting, 43–44; social centers and, 48, 70–71

Stockholm. Autonomous scene in, 114–118, 124–127; gentrification in, 114, 116; history, 21; Södermalm borough, 114–117, 132–133; suburbs, 117–118;

submerged networks, 9

Svenska Dagbladet (newspaper), 54, 158

Sydsvenskan (newspaper), 51, 57, 82

syndicalism, 32, 35, 43, 63, 142, 159

Sweden. Autonomous movements in, 28–29, 103; as case study, 5–6, 17–19;

gentrification in, 5–7,19–23, 41–42, 82–89; myths about, 6, 18–19, 29, 44–46; people's home (folkhemmet),33–34, 44–46; political culture, 28–34; social movement history, 34–44; Swedishness, 25, 48–49, 79, 103, 148

tactics. Building new places, 69–72, 96–98, 135; city as living room, 4–5, 92–95, 152; creativity and, 96–99, 103; diversity of, 128; street festivals, 4–5, 89–96, 102

temporality 11, 15, 23, 70, 73, 97, 100, 112, 153, 156; agency and, 153; future research and, 156; language and, 69–78; momentum, 100, 112, 138, 153; projectivity 11, 15, 23, 70, 73, 97, 100, 153; squatting and, 138–139; volition, 154–155

territory 1–3, 13, 99

Ungdomshuset (Copenhagen). See social centers

use value, 12

Utkanten (Malmö). See social centers

welfare state. Folk movements and, 30–34; political culture and, 29; Take Back Welfare Campaign, 45–46; welfare retrenchment, 17–19, 44–45

Women. See gender

Kimberly A. Creasap is a sociologist and Director of the Susan Hirt Hagen Center for Civic and Urban Engagement at Wittenberg University.

www.ingramcontent.com/pod-product-compliance
Lightning Source LLC
Chambersburg PA
CBHW020704270326
41928CB00005B/261